PENGUIN BOOKS

Life and Laughing

Life and Laughing

My Story

MICHAEL McINTYRE

PENGUIN BOOKS

PENGUIN BOOKS

Published by the Penguin Group
Penguin Books Ltd, 80 Strand, London WC2R ORL, England
Penguin Group (USA) Inc., 375 Hudson Street, New York, New York 10014, USA
Penguin Group (Canada), 90 Eglinton Avenue East, Suite 700, Toronto, Ontario, Canada M4P 2Y3
(a division of Pearson Penguin Canada Inc.)
Penguin Ireland, 25 St Stephen's Green, Dublin 2, Ireland (a division of Penguin Books Ltd)
Penguin Group (Australia), 250 Camberwell Road, Camberwell, Victoria 3124, Australia
(a division of Pearson Australia Group Pty Ltd)
Penguin Books India Pvt Ltd, 11 Community Centre, Panchsheel Park, New Delhi – 110 017, India
Penguin Group (NZ), 67 Apollo Drive, Rosedale, Auckland 0632, New Zealand
(a division of Pearson New Zealand Ltd)
Penguin Books (South Africa) (Pty) Ltd, 24 Sturdee Avenue, Rosebank,
Johannesburg 2196, South Africa

Penguin Books Ltd, Registered Offices: 80 Strand, London WC2R ORL, England

www.penguin.com
First published by Michael Joseph 2010
Published in Penguin Books 2011

024

Copyright © Michael McIntyre, 2010
All rights reserved

The moral right of the author has been asserted

All images courtesy of the author except: Fremantle Media (Michael's father with Kenny Everett and
Barry Cryer); © The *Sun* and 01.06.1984/nisyndication.com (Newspaper clipping of Michael's mother with
Kenny Everett); Richard Young/Rex Features (Michael with his wife at the *GQ* Awards); Dave M. Benett/
Getty Images (Michael with Ronnie Corbett, Rob Brydon and Billy Connolly); Ken McKay/Rex Features
(Michael with Prince Charles); Ellis O'Brien (DVD advert at Piccadilly Circus, Michael on stage at the
Comedy Roadshow, Michael on stage at Wembley)

Set in Garamond MT Std 12.5/14.75 pt
Typeset by Palimpsest Book Production Limited, Falkirk, Stirlingshire

Printed in Great Britain by Clays Ltd, Elcograf S.p.A.

ISBN: 978-0-141-04567-2

www.greenpenguin.co.uk

Penguin Books is committed to a sustainable
future for our business, our readers and our planet.
This book is made from Forest Stewardship
Council™ certified paper.

For Kitty, Lucas and Oscar

I

I am writing this on my new 27-inch iMac. I have ditched my PC and gone Mac. I was PC for years, but Microsoft Word kept criticizing my grammar, and I think it started to affect my self-esteem. It had a lot of issues with a lot of my sentences, and after years of its making me feel stupid I ended the relationship and bought a Mac. It's gorgeous and enormous, and I bought it especially to write my book (the one you're reading now). For the last six months, I've been looking to create the perfect writing environment. Aside from the computer, I have a new desk, a new chair and a new office with newly painted walls in my new house.

When my wife and I were looking at houses, she would be busily opening and closing cupboards and chattering about storage (after a few months of house-hunting, I became convinced my wife's dream home would be the Big Yellow Storage Company), and I would be searching for the room to write my book. The view seemed very important. Previously, views hadn't been that important to me. I prefer TV. Views only really have one channel. But suddenly I was very keen to find a room with a view to inspire me to write a classic autobiography. Like David Niven's, but about my life and not his.

The house we fell in love with had a room with a beautiful view of the garden and even a balcony for closer viewing of the view of the garden. It was a room with a view. It was perfect. I could create magic in this room. Soon after moving in, I plonked my desk directly in front of the balcony window. I stood behind the desk drinking in the view of my garden and thought, 'I need a new chair', a throne of creativity. With this view and the right chair, I can't possibly fail.

The big question when office chair purchasing is 'to swivel or not to swivel?' I would love to find out how many of the great literary works of the twentieth century have been written by swivelling writers. Were D. H. Lawrence, J. R. R. Tolkien or Virginia Woolf slightly dizzy when they penned their finest works? I tried out several swivel chairs in Habitat on the Finchley Road for so long that I got told off. I realized a swivel chair would be a mistake. I'd have too much fun. I might as well put a slide, a seesaw or a bouncy castle in my office. So I settled on a chair whose biggest selling feature was that you can sit on it.

With my chair, desk and view sorted, it was time to address the décor. The previous owner had painted the walls of my new office orange. I'll try to be more specific. They were Tangerine. No, they were more a Clementine or maybe a Mandarin. Come to think of it, they were Satsuma. Now, there was no way on God's earth I could write this book with a Satsuma backdrop, so I went to Farrow & Ball on Hampstead's high street. Farrow & Ball is the latest in a long line of successful high street double acts (Marks & Spencer, Dolce & Gabbana, Bang & Olufsen). It's basically paint for posh people. I don't know who Farrow was, or indeed Ball, but I bet they were posh. Maybe I'm wrong. Maybe Ball is Bobby Ball from Cannon and Ball, who tried his luck in the paint industry encouraged by Cannon's success manufacturing cameras.

I perused the colour chart in Farrow & Ball. There are so many colours, it makes you go a bit mad trying to decide. It's also very hard to distinguish between many of them. A quick googling of the Farrow & Ball colour chart reveals ten different shades of white. All White, Strong White, House White, New White, White Tie . . . you get the idea. I once bought a white sofa from DFS. It was white. If you asked a hundred people what colour it was, I would say that a hundred of them would say it was white. In actual fact, they would all be wrong; it was Montana Ice. I would suggest that even if you asked a hundred Montanans during a particularly cold winter what colour it was, they would say, 'White.'

After a brief discussion with my wife (she's actually colour-blind, but I find it hard to reach decisions on my own), I popped for the unmistakable colour of Brinjal No. 222. A slightly less pretentious description would be aubergine. Most people call it purple.

My surroundings were now nearly complete: new desk, new chair, lovely view and Brinjal No. 222 walls. I placed my Mac on the desk and lovingly peeled off the see-through plastic that protects the screen, took a deep breath and sat down. Unfortunately 27 inches of screen meant that my view was completely obscured. Panic. Why didn't I think of that? The whole window was blocked by this enormous piece of technology. I was forced to move the desk to the opposite wall. I now had a face full of Brinjal No. 222 and my back to the view. I would have to turn the chair around at regular intervals to be inspired by my view. I should have bought the swivel chair.

OK, I'm ready. I'm ready to start my book. It's an auto-biography, although I prefer the word 'memoirs'. I think it's from the French for 'memories', and that pretty much sums up what this book is going to be. A book about my French memories. No, it's basically everything I can remember from my life. The bad news is that I don't have a particularly good memory. You know when someone asks you what you did yesterday, and it takes you ages to remember even though it was just one day ago – 'I can't believe this, it was just yesterday', you'll say before finally remembering. Well, I'm like that, except sometimes it never comes to me. I never remember what I did yesterday. Come to think of it, what did I do yesterday?

'Memoirs' just sounds a lot sexier than 'autobiography'. Not all words are better in French. 'Swimming pool' in French is *piscine*, which obviously sounds like 'piss in'. 'Do you piscine the piscine?' was as funny as French lessons at school ever got for me. Only writing BOOB on a calculator using 8008 in Maths seemed funnier. We've borrowed loads of French words to spice up the English language: fiancé, encore, cul-de-sac, apéritif, chauffeur, pied-à-terre, déjà vu. In fact, you could probably speak an entire English sentence with more French in it than English. 'I'm having *apéritifs* and *hors d'oeuvres* at my *pied-à-terre* in a *cul-de-sac*. After some *mangetouts*, I'm sending the kids to the *crèche* and having a *ménage à trois* with my *fiancée* and the *au pair*.' Sounds like a great night.

The good news is I think there's more than enough in my patchy memory for the book. Whatever the French for 'patchy memories' is, that's what this book is. So where better to start than with my earliest memory? I was at a pre-school called Stepping Stones in North London in a class called the Dolphins. I must have been about four years old. I remember it being some kind of music group. We were all in a circle with instruments. I may have had a xylophone, but I can't be sure. What I do remember is that there was the distinct smell of shit in the room. At this age kids are toilet-trained, so whereas only a couple years previously at nursery or playgroup the smell of shit was a given, in this environment it was unwelcome.

The simple fact was, a four-year-old kid had taken a shit in his or her little pants. It wasn't me. I have never pooed my pants, although as this was my earliest memory, I can't be sure. I remember trying to ignore the smell of shit and just get on with what I was doing, much like being on the top deck of a night bus.

'I smell poo,' said the teacher. Cue hysterical giggling. 'Please tell me if you think it might be you. You're not in trouble.'

Nobody responded. A chubby boy holding a triangle looked slightly guilty to me. A blonde girl with a bongo also looked a bit sheepish.

The teacher enquired again. No response. A third time she asked. You could cut the pungent atmosphere with some safety scissors.

Still nobody came clean about their dirty little secret. Then the teacher announced something that I think is the reason I remember this moment still to this day. She said that if nobody would own up, then everyone must, in turn, pull their pants down to prove it.

Horror. I couldn't believe this. How humiliating. In fact the thought of it nearly made me shit myself. A Chinese kid gasped and dropped his tambourine. One by one, around the circle, we had to stand up and reveal our bottoms to the music group. The tension may have damaged me for life. I remember this unbearable swelling of fear as my turn approached. I frantically scanned the room for the crapping culprit. I ruled out the teacher, although I had my doubts about the elderly woman on the piano. I pinned my hopes on this kid who had a permanently solidified snotty nose. I think everyone can recall the kid in their class at pre-school with a permanently solidified snotty nose. Well, my class had one. He was about four kids to my right, and I prayed it wasn't just the nose area he'd let himself down in.

My prime suspect stood up, seemingly in slow motion, and burst into tears. It WAS him! Thank God. I was saved, but the experience has been permanently etched on my mind. Incidentally, if you were in that circle and were one of the kids who had to pull their pants down, please get in touch. I'd love to know how your life turned out.

It is odd how we remember scenes from our childhood at random. Your first few years are, of course, a total blank. I've got two sons, who are four years and one year old, and they aren't going to remember any of their lives so far. I was going to take them to a museum today. Why bother? I might just send them to their rooms until they're old enough to remember some of this effort I'm putting in.

So everything prior to Poo-gate is a mystery to me. I have to rely on my parents, old photographs and Wikipedia to fill me in. According to Wikipedia, I was born in 1976 on 15 February. However, according to my mother, it was 21 February 1976. I don't know who to believe. One thing they both agree on is that I was born in Merton. I think that's in South London. I'm flabbergasted by this news as I am a North Londoner through and through. My opinion about South London is exactly the same as the opinion of South Londoners towards North London: 'How can you live there? It's weird.' I get a chill when I drive over Hammersmith Bridge. I feel as though I'm entering a different world. I wonder if I need a passport and check that my mobile phone still has a signal. The roads seem to be too wide, they don't have parks, they have 'commons', and everyone looks a bit like Tim Henman's dad.

(I've just realized that I have to be careful about how much personal information I reveal. I think there's already enough to answer most of the security questions at my bank and get access to all my accounts.)

I have details about my birth from my mother, who says she was there for most of it. I weighed 8 pounds and 11 ounces. I'm telling you that because the weight of babies seems very important to people. No other measurement is of interest: height, width, circumference – couldn't give a shit. But the weight is must-have information.

I was a big baby. My mother tells me this, and so does everyone else when they learn of my opening weight. Like it was my fault, I let myself go, I could have done with losing a few ounces, a little less 'womb service' and a little more swimming and maybe those newborn nappies wouldn't have been so tight.

Not only was I a big baby, I was also remarkably oriental in appearance. Nobody really knows why I looked like Mr Miyagi from *The Karate Kid* and, let's be honest, my appearance has been the source of quite a lot of material for me. A midwife asked my mother if my father was Chinese or Japanese. My grandparents thought my parents took home the wrong baby. Questions were asked about my mother's fidelity. My father beat up our local dry cleaner, Mr Wu.

Every year I, like you, celebrate my own birth and the fact that I am still alive on my birthday. This is always a very emotional day for my mother, who annually telephones me throughout the day reliving my birth. She calls without fail at about 3 a.m. telling me that this is when her waters broke, and I get phoned throughout the morning and afternoon with her updating me on how far apart her contractions were. At 5.34 p.m., I get my final phone call announcing my birth, and then she reminds me that I was '8 pounds 11 ounces, a very big baby'.

Since I became a comedian, she now adds that the labour ward was also the scene of my very first joke. Apparently, when I was only a few minutes old, the doctor lay me down to give me a quick examination, and I promptly peed all over him. I'm told it got a big laugh from the small audience that included my mother, father, the midwife and the doctor. Knowing me, I probably laughed too.

It was the first laugh I ever got.

2

Why do I look foreign? Let's examine my heritage. My parents are not English people. My father is from Montreal in Canada, and both my mother's parents were from Hungary. I am therefore a 'Canary'. I consider myself British. I have only visited Hungary and Canada once.

My one and only visit to Hungary was with my grandmother and my sister Lucy. I was twenty years old, Lucy was eighteen and my grandma was seventy-nine. My grandmother was an eccentric woman, to say the least. Think Zsa Zsa Gabor or Ivana Trump, and you wouldn't be too far out. She was funny, glamorous and rich. A true character. I will do my best to convey her accent when I quote her.

'Helllow, daaarling', that kind of thing.

This is actually how she wrote English as well as spoke it. Born in Budapest, she claims to have 'rrun avay vith the circuss' as a child before marrying scientist Laszlo Katz. When the Nazis showed up in 1939, they fled their home country and settled in Roehampton, South London (I would have taken my chances with the Nazis). They lived in a Tudor house. You know, white with black beams. Well, according to my mother, my grandma painted the black beams bright blue until the council made her paint them black again three weeks later. She didn't speak a word of English when she arrived and learned it from eavesdropping and watching television, much like *E.T.* or Daryl Hannah in *Splash*.

My grandmother was undoubtedly a bright cookie, and her vocabulary soon increased enough for her to get by. However, her accent would still hold her back. Trying to buy haddock at her local fishmonger's, she would ask politely, 'Do you hev a heddek?'

Unfortunately, the fishmonger thought she was saying, 'Do you have a headache?'

'No, I'm fine, thank you, love,' he would reply. He thought she was a nutty foreign lady enquiring after his well-being. He was only half right.

The headache/haddock misunderstanding occurred several times until my grandmother burst into tears in her blue Tudor house. She asked her husband through her sobs, 'Vot iz it vith dis cuntry, vy vont dey give me a heddek?'

My grandfather, whose accent was no better, stormed round to the fishmonger's. He called the fishmonger a racist and demanded to know why he didn't give his wife a 'headache' when there were several 'headaches' in the window. Luckily, the mistake was realized before they came to blows, which would have resulted in one of them having a genuine 'heddek'.

My grandmother soon became fluent in English, so

much so that she became quite the best Scrabble player I've ever encountered. She was even better than the 'Difficult' setting on the Scrabble App for my iPhone and would repeatedly beat her second husband, Jim, a Cambridge-educated Englishman. She was not only a tremendously talented Scrabbler, but also fiercely competitive and uncharacteristically arrogant when involved in a game, often calling me a 'loozer' or claiming she was going to give me a good 'vipping' or exclaiming, 'Yuv got nothing, English boy!'

I enjoyed countless games of Scrabble with her in my late teens and early twenties. Not only did I enjoy the games, but there were serious financial rewards. You see, the Cambridge-educated Englishman was loaded, having made a fortune as a stockbroker. After his untimely death, my glamour gran was left to fend for herself. So I would visit her, and we would play Scrabble. If I won, she would give me a crisp £50 note, and if I lost, she would give me a crisp £50 note. So you see how this was quite an attractive proposition for a poor student. A lot of my friends were working as waiters and in telesales to make extra money, whereas I was playing Scrabble with my grandma at least five times a week.

You might wonder where these £50 notes were coming from. Well, my glamour gran didn't really trust banks, so when her husband died, she withdrew a lot of money and kept it hidden around her lavish apartment in Putney. I'd open a cupboard in the kitchen looking for a mug and find one at the back packed with fifties. I once found 400 quid in a flannel next to the bath and two squashed fifties when I changed the batteries in her TV remote control.

K5 E1 R1 R1 I1 T1 Z10

'Triple vurd score and "E" is on a duble letteer, so that's sixty-six points. Read it and veep, loozer,' said my grandmother in a particularly competitive mood as she stretched her lead.

Now, although she was a wonderfully gifted word-smith in her second language, she never learned how to spell many of the words. Often she would get a word that bore no resemblance to the one she was attempting. The best of which was undoubtedly 'Kerritz'. It was a sensational Scrabble word. To use the Z and K on a triple letter score and score sixty-six – exceptional. The only problem was that outside of her mind the word was fictitious. It soon transpired that only the two Rs were correct and that the actual word she was attempting was 'carrots'. I must have laughed for about half an hour.

If I'm honest, I've never really been that into history, neither of the world nor of my ancestors. I hadn't asked many questions about my Hungarian ancestry, and I suppose I must have tuned out if it was ever mentioned prior to my Budapest trip. But the time had come. My grandmother, sister and I were off to half my family's homeland. Astonishingly, nobody had mentioned to me or my sister that we still had family in Hungary; nor did they mention that they were Jewish.

So when we were met at Budapest airport by a man resembling a stocky Jesus Christ, I assumed he was the cab driver. When he kissed me and my sister all over our faces, I assumed he was quite the friendliest cab driver I had ever encountered. When Grandma told us he wasn't the cab driver, I thought for a fleeting moment it was Jesus.

'Heelloo, I im yur Unkal Peeeteer.' His accent was worse than my grandmother's.

It turned out Uncle Peter was the son of my real grandfather's sister, my real grandfather being Laszlo Katz, the Hungarian scientist, and not Jim, the rich English stockbroker who was my grandmother's second husband and the man who enabled us to afford the Hyatt Regency Hotel, Budapest. Are you following this? I'm not and couldn't at the time.

Uncle Peter was Jewish. There was no mistaking that. He had the hair and beard of the Messiah and a trait that is stereotypically shared by Jewish men. He had a nose nearly the size of the plane we'd just got off. I didn't know I had Jewish blood; I always thought that my grandfather was Catholic. In fact, he was. He changed his faith, as Judaism wasn't all that trendy circa 1940. But nobody told me.

Suddenly I'm Jewish. I instantly started to feel more

neurotic and speak with the rhythm of Jackie Mason. I turned to my grandmother, 'Oy vey, why did you not tell me already? I thought I was Gentile, but I have Jewish blood pumping through my veins. Did you not have the chutzpah to tell me? Did you think I was such a klutz I couldn't cope with it? You wait till we schlep all the way over here, treating me like a nebbish. This is all too much, I have a headache.'

'Vy have you bought a heddek? Did yu not eat enuf on de plane that you need to smuggel fish? And we just valked through "Nuuthing to declare"!'

Uncle Peter was so pleased to see Lucy and me that it became quite emotional. His mother, Auntie Yoli, and he were the last remaining family in Hungary after the horrors of the war. By Hungarian standards, Peter had done very well for himself. I can't remember exactly what he did, but I know there was a factory involved. He spoke good English and had love in his eyes. But looking at him, I could not help but wonder how I could possibly be related to the man.

In the car park we approached his 4x4. It was by far the most luxurious car on display. 'Shtopp!' hollered Peter, much like the man from the Grolsch adverts. He then took out his keys, pointed a device through the window and waited for a beep. 'It is now safe to enter.' Safe? What was he talking about? 'You must vait for mi to disingage the sacurrity system,' he continued, 'othurwide, verrrryy dangeruss.'

'Isn't it just an alarm?' I asked.

'No, iiit iz gas.'

'Gas? What do you mean?'

'In Hungarry is verrry meny criimes. So if break in my caar, you get gas in fece, verry bed burning in eyes. Blind for meny minnuts,' he said, quite matter-of-fact.

'You can gas burglars in the face here? What happens if you forget to disengage it and open the car door?'

'I have bin in hosspitaal three times!'

It turned out he had forgotten to turn off his car security system and, on three occasions gassed himself in the face. Each time he was hospitalized. In fact one time, while he was rolling around on the pavement in agony holding his eyes and screaming, somebody had casually taken his keys and nicked his stereo.

It was on hearing this that I was convinced. We are related.

I spent three days learning a lot about Budapest and my family. Unfortunately, the only thing I really remember is Peter gassing himself in the face – oh, and that he had green leather sofas. Hideous. Maybe the self-gassing affected his sight.

I have been to Montreal, my father's birthplace, only once. As has been reported at length in every *Daily Mail* interview I've done, my father died when I was seventeen years old. I recently did interviews with the *Daily Mail* and *Heat* magazine back to back in a hotel in

Manchester. The *Mail* grilled me at length about the passing of my dad until I had tears in my eyes. The interview ended, the tape recorder stopped, my tears were wiped, and the *Mail* journalist was replaced by the one from *Heat*, whose first question was 'How do you get your hair so bouncy?', at which point my publicist jumped in: 'Michael doesn't want to answer any personal questions.'

I was in Montreal for the Comedy Festival a few years ago. Montreal is split into French- and English-speakers, and as you can imagine, they don't really get on. My first introduction to French in Montreal was an unfortunate incident in my hotel shower. When the letter 'C' is on a tap, I normally feel pretty confident I'm reaching for the 'Cold' tap. However, 'C' on French taps stands for 'Chaud' which means 'Hot'. I turned up the 'Chaud', thinking it was 'Cold'. When the water got hotter, I simply added more 'Chaud'. I was scalded.

This wasn't the only Anglo-French misunderstanding I encountered in Canada. When businessmen are on the road, often the only highlight is watching pornography in hotel rooms. Sad but true. In fact, checking out of a hotel can feel a bit like confession. 'Forgive me, Novotel Leeds receptionist, for I have sinned; I watched four pornos. I also had two Toblerones, the Maltesers, the sour cream and chive Pringles and five miniature Cognacs from the mini-bar. And I have one of your towels in my bag.'

Checking in to my Montreal hotel, I had a few hours to kill until the gig so, and I apologize to younger readers, I was contemplating the potentially higher calibre of Canadian 'adult' entertainment awaiting me in room 417. The receptionist handed me the key for my room and then enquired whether it was the only key I required.

'Do you want one key?' she asked. However, in her thick French accent this became 'Do you want wanky?' I was startled to say the least. What kind of a hotel was this? I immediately went to my room for a cold shower, but as you know scalded myself.

Being in Montreal, I naturally felt nostalgic for my dad, but, unlike my trip to Hungary, I was alone. I sent an email to my father's brother, Hazen. The last I had heard from him was that he was playing a cross-dresser in a Chinese sitcom (my family have had varying degrees of success in showbusiness). In the last twenty years, I had had lunch with him once, when he visited London. It was eerie as he shared mannerisms with my father, as well as his accent and intonations.

Hazen had remarried, to a seemingly sweet Chinese lady who smiled politely through lunch as Hazen reminisced about my dad. He literally didn't stop talking while his spaghetti meatballs went cold in Café Pasta just off Oxford Street. His wife never spoke. 'In all the years we've been married, she's only ever said thirty-seven words to me. Two of them were "I do."' He was funny. He spoke about my father's dry sense of humour and how in the early sixties my dad had come to London as a comedian in search of stardom. And here I was, back in his native Montreal doing the same thing.

In his email, Hazen told me about the neighbourhood where he and my dad grew up in the fifties and places they used to go as kids. In particular, he mentioned my dad's favourite deli. I searched for the neighbourhood and the deli on a map given to me by the concierge. Having located the deli, I was all set to go when I had second thoughts about my sentimental sojourn. I imagined a bustling deli full of lunching Canadians and wondered what I would gain by eating a pastrami sandwich on my own among them. The fact is, my dad wasn't going to be there.

But he lived on in me and he also lived on in his other kids. Aside from my sister Lucy, my dad had two further children after my parents divorced, Billy and Georgina, both of whom I had had very little contact with since my father died. So I found them on Myspace (my computer just underlined Myspace in red and suggested I meant Facebook. Apple iMacs are so cool) and sent messages.

Within hours they both got back to me. Billy, it transpired, was in Vermont for the summer. A mere three hours' drive. A few hours later, there was a knock on my hotel room door and standing there was my father's son, Billy McIntyre. Billy was an all-American kid. He was twenty years old, the lead singer in a band and good-looking. In short, nothing like me. We shared a special few days together that I'm sure would have meant more to our dad than me sitting alone in his favourite deli.

I was in Montreal primarily to work, so Billy came with me to a number of my shows. I introduced him to my fellow comedians as 'my long-lost brother', not realizing that this seemed dubious to say the least. It soon got back to me that the word was I was a homosexual. It looked for all the world as if I had picked up a local rent boy. It never crossed my mind how strange it seemed that I was suddenly hanging around with this young American kid who was also sleeping in my room.

All of the comedians were staying in the same hotel. Billy and I would walk past a gaggle of gagsters who would stop their conversation and stare, muttering to each other about the shameless exhibiting of my new sexual direction. To me, it was an emotional reunion; to everybody else, it was like a gay version of the film *Pretty Woman*.

On my last day of the Festival, I was in the lobby saying goodbye to Billy and slipped him a few hundred quid. It was the big brotherly thing to do, but at this very moment Frank Skinner walked past and gave me a knowing nod. I must admit; it didn't look good.

3

Now, older readers all remember the year of my birth. Not because my entering the world made international news headlines:

CHINESE TAKEAWAY! BRITISH PARENTS TAKE HOME ORIENTAL BABY

It's because 1976 was the last baking hot summer. It has become a legendary year, referenced by middle-aged Brits every time there is a heat wave (two hot days in a row), a mini-heat wave (one hot day in a row) or a micro-heat wave (the sun comes out between two clouds). This just winds me up as every spring I, like you, yearn for a long hot summer that never materializes. Well, it turns out I was actually alive for the best summer of them all. London was scorching and everyone was brown (although I was yellow due to jaundice). It was my first experience of weather and it was fantastic. I thought I lived in California, my mother didn't need to buy me clothes for eight months, my first word was 'Nivea'.

In truth, the heat wave of 1976 was probably greatly exaggerated. In future years when we talk about the winter we've just endured, we'll probably add a few inches of snow and deduct a few degrees from the temperature and the wind chill factor. When our grandchildren are longing for snow, we will wax lyrical about the snow of 2010 (of course, when I am a grandparent, I will then look almost exactly like Mr Miyagi so I will 'Wax lyrical ON, Wax lyrical OFF' about the snow of 2010*):

'The blizzard lasted six long weeks. Sixteen feet of snow fell solidly. They were using a blank white sheet of paper for the weather forecast. Cars, houses, entire villages, disappeared. The whole country was housebound apart from Torvill and Dean, and Omar Sharif, who had experienced similar conditions during his portrayal of Dr Zhivago.'

I think Sharif would also have coped well in the heat wave of 1976, thanks to his sterling work on *Lawrence of Arabia*. Anyway, this isn't Omar Sharif's autobiography, it's mine, so let's get back to it. I'm born, it's hot, and I move into a tiny flat with my parents in Kensington Church Street, London. My birth certificate states that at the time my father was a 'Record producer'. I know bits about his career in comedy, but little about his days in the music industry other than that he had one big hit,

---

* This joke requires the viewing of *The Karate Kid*, the original film starring Ralph Macchio.

the novelty record 'Grandad' by Clive Dunn, which was number 1 for three weeks in 1971.

My mother, who has produced no novelty records about family members, was beautiful. I'm basing this on old photographs. In every one, she looks stunning, but let's be honest, she would have weeded out any less than flattering photos over the years and destroyed them. This is what women do; they constantly edit their photo albums so that history may remember them looking their best. Old people basically get the best photo from their youth and use it as a sort of publicity shot – 'Look at me, I could have been a model, I had an 18-inch waist, I got asked for ID at the pictures when I was thirty-two.' That's the great thing about being old – you can say what you like to your grandkids. Not only because they weren't there, but also because they're not really listening.

Personally, I am particularly un-photogenic. Cruelly, it is suggested that people who are not photogenic are ugly. I had some stand-up material along those lines about passport photos and how people hide them claiming, 'It's a terrible photo, I'm really ugly in it, I don't look anything like this.'

If this was true, they wouldn't get past immigration, but the fact is they do. The immigration guy never says, 'You don't look anything like this photo. This photo is of an ugly person. You, on the other hand, have a sculpted beauty that brings to mind a young Brando. I will not let you into this country, you gorgeous liar.' No, they look at your ugly photo and then look at your ugly face and let you go to baggage reclaim.

I've been lucky enough to be photographed by some seasoned snappers, but it is very difficult to get a good shot of me. I would say that I am happy with about 1 in 10 photos of me. I would say that my wife is happy with maybe 4 in 10 photos of her. Therefore the odds of getting a good photo of us together are 0.4 in 10 (I wasn't just reading the word 'BOOB' on my calculator in Maths). To put it another way: very unlikely. The odds on a family photo where my wife, our two boys and I look good all at the same time: impossible. The result is that there are very few photos of my wife and me together that haven't been deleted or destroyed by one of us.

To get a photo of my wife and me together, some-body else has to take it. On our honeymoon in the Maldives, we kept taking photos of each other; me in bed alone, her swimming alone, me in a hammock alone, her in a jacuzzi alone. The woman in Boots, Brent Cross, developing our holiday snaps must have thought we'd each gone on an 18–30 singles holiday and not pulled. Who was I supposed to ask to take our photo? I've never really taken to asking waiters when you have to explain that your camera works in exactly the same way as every other camera on earth – 'it's the button on the right' – and it still takes them so long to work it out that you develop a slightly annoyed smirk, ruining the photo.

Having no photos of us together on our honeymoon simply wouldn't do. So on the last day when I had one photo remaining on our disposable camera, I asked a sweet gentleman called Nizoo who was delivering room service if he could take a photo. 'Of course,' he agreed, before standing up as straight as he could and smiling inanely at us. He was under the misapprehension that we wanted to photograph him. I didn't have the heart to tell him that it was us I wanted him to photograph. The upshot is that the only couple who appear in my honeymoon photos are Nizoo and myself.

I imagine the woman in Boots, Brent Cross, sitting in the darkroom thinking, 'Ah, sweet, he met someone right at the end.'

My mother may also have looked good in 1976 because she was nineteen years old. Yes, I am the result of a teenage pregnancy. My father, on the other hand, was thirty-seven. He was a cradle snatcher, which was good for me as I was now sleeping in the vacated cradle. Thirty-seven! That's four years older than I am now, and I'm writing my autobiography. He had a whole life before me. Born, as you know, in Montreal, he was named Thomas Cameron McIntyre, but changed his name to Ray Cameron to make this book slightly more confusing. Ray Cameron was his stage name. My mum called him Cameron, showbiz associates called him

Ray, his mother called him Tommy and I called him Dad.

He decided that he'd have a better shot at fame and fortune with a new name. Loads of celebs have changed their name. In most cases I think artists would have found the same success with their original names: Elton John (Reginald Dwight), Cliff Richard (Harry Webb), Kenny Everett (Maurice Cole), Michael Caine (Maurice Micklewhite), Tina Turner (Anna Bullock), Omar Sharif (Michael Shalhoub – I'm obsessed with him today), Meatloaf (Steak Sandwich – I made this one up). In some cases, however, you can see why a change was necessary. Would you have been comfortable listening to 'Wonderful Tonight' by Eric Clapp? Laughing at *Fawlty Towers* with John Cheese? Or watching *Newsnight* with Jeremy Fuxmen (I made this one up, too)?

According to his brother Hazen, when we chatted in Café Pasta, the young Thomas McIntyre originally wanted to be a singer, but suffered a serious throat infection (I don't remember the details) in his teens. He lost his voice for months, communicating by writing things down. Apparently he already had a wonderfully dry sense of humour, but his time spent voiceless meant he couldn't waste any words when communicating through notes. This sharpened his comedy mind, and he often presented notes that had surrounding Canadian people in stitches. When he could speak again, his singing voice was lost, but his comedy voice was found. He started to perform stand-up locally with success before crossing the pond to try his luck in the bright lights of London. This might be a romanticized version of events, but I like it, so I'm going with it.

In the early Swinging Sixties, my father, who was in his early swinging twenties, was performing live comedy in swinging London. The sixties stand-up scene was very different to what it is today. There were no comedy clubs. This was the age of cabaret and variety. My dad was the MC, introducing dancing girls and novelty acts while telling jokes in between. I feel extremely lucky to have some of his actual scripts. Only one of them, dated 11 November 1962, mentions a venue, the nightclub Whisky a Go Go. I researched it thoroughly (typed it into Google) and it seems to have been the original name of the Wag Club in Wardour Street and is described as a 'late-night dive bar'. The office for Open Mike Productions, who make *Live at the Apollo* and *Michael McIntyre's Comedy Roadshow*, is just a few doors down Wardour Street. In the last few years, I have spent countless days working there.

In fact, I've probably spent more time than I should have at the Wardour Street office. This is mainly due to Itsu, the sushi restaurant at number 103. I'm a big fan of raw fish. Although Itsu itself is synonymous with poisoning Russian spies with Polonium-210, the sushi that doesn't contain radiation is divine, particularly the scallops. Itsu has one of those carousels, where you sit down and the food just passes by you: salmon, tuna, squid, miso soup, edamame beans. I once saw a Samsonite holdall around the time Terminal 5 opened at Heathrow. You pick what you want from colour-coded plates that relate to their price, and I literally cannot stop eating. My rule is that once the plates are piled up so high that I cannot see the carousel, I should probably get the bill.

I'm glad there isn't an Itsu closer to home. You know the expression 'There are plenty more fish in the sea'? Well, I don't think that's the case any more. What I don't understand about the Russian spy murderers is, how did they know he was going to pick the Polonium-poisoned piece from the carousel? Maybe they just wanted to kill somebody at random. Like Russian roulette, they poisoned one piece of sushi and watched it go round and round the carousel waiting for one unlucky luncher to select it. It could have been some advertising exec but ended up being a Russian spy. I don't know. What I do know is that it's a bloody cheek having 12.5 per cent service included in the bill. I picked the dishes off the carousel and brought them to my table. The waiter only takes them away. I figure this is worth a maximum of 6 per cent.

It's incredible to think that as I sit in Itsu arguing over the service charge in front of a tower of empty plates resembling the Burj Khalifa building in Dubai, fifty years earlier my dad was performing just a few yards away, clutching these very notes I have in my hand today.

It's fascinating for me to see my dad's notes. A comedian's notes tend to make little sense. They will consist of subject headings and key words. My dad's notes say things like 'Westminster Abbey', 'School teacher', 'The house bit' and 'Your horse has diabetes . . .' Comedians carry around these scribbles of key words that they hope contain the DNA of a good gag. Looking at some of the notes from my last tour, it's the same kind of thing: 'Wrinkle cream', 'Morning', 'Last day sunbathing'. I once thought it would be fun to swap notes with other comics on the bill and try to make jokes about each other's subjects onstage. This suggestion wasn't met with much enthusiasm in Jongleurs, Leeds, circa 2005.

In among the notes there is a script, and it's hilarious. So here's my dad in a Soho nightclub in 1962:

I'd like to tell you a bit about myself . . . I'm one of the better lower priced performers . . . I'm from Canada. I realize that it may be a little difficult because you've never heard of me here but don't let it worry you 'cause I have the same problem in Canada . . .

But it's real nice to be here . . . I brought my wife over with me . . . You know how it is . . . You always pack a few things you don't need . . .

We had a very interesting flight over here, we came on a

non-scheduled airline . . . You know what that is? . . . That's the type of airline who aren't sure when the crash is going to be . . . You see, they use old planes . . . In fact this one was so old that the 'No Smoking' sign came on in Latin . . .

But don't get me wrong it wasn't all bad . . . There were only a few things that I didn't like . . . For instance when I fly I like to have . . . Two wings . . .

It's such a treat to have so many attractive ladies in the audience . . . Especially for me . . . Because I come from a very small town . . . And I don't want to say the girls in my home town were ugly, but we had a beauty contest there once . . . And nobody won . . .

They finally picked one girl and called her the winner, actually she wasn't that bad . . . She had a beautiful bone structure in her face . . . Those eyes . . . Those lips . . . That tooth . . . She had this one tooth right in the front and it was three inches long . . . The first time I saw her I thought it was a cigarette and tried to light it . . . To see her eating spaghetti was really something . . . She used to put her tooth right in it and spin the plate . . . But I married her anyway . . .

I got married because I wanted to have a family and it wasn't long before we had the pitter-patter of tiny feet around the house . . . My mother-in-law's a midget . . . I told her to treat the house as if it were her own . . . And she did. She sold it . . .

I hope you found that as funny as I did. I particularly like the 'I thought it was a cigarette and tried to light it' bit.

This is proper old-school stuff, wives and mother-in-laws being the butt of the joke. I don't know if he wrote all of it, some of it or none of it. I know that comedians back in those days used to share jokes around a lot, but nevertheless it's still funny. I have gags, I couldn't really survive without punchlines, but a lot of my material is observational or mimicry. It's a different approach to making people laugh – it makes me laugh, which is why I say it. But you can understand how 'old-school' comedians can be baffled by 'alternative' comedy, because there are so few proper 'gags'. 'Where are the jokes?' they'll say, normally in a northern accent. For me, it's quite simple: if people are laughing, it's comedy . . . or tickling.

Browsing my dad's notes, I'm not sure he was the most confident performer. There are two pages entitled 'No Laughs', back-up in case the jokes weren't working. Here are some of them:

Well, I wasn't born here, but I'm certainly dying here.

That gag is twenty years ahead of its time. It's just your bad luck that you had to hear it tonight.

Well, from now on, it's a comeback.

I don't mind you going to sleep, but you could at least say goodnight.

Ouch. I certainly never had a plan for dying onstage. I've always found that once you've lost an audience, there's nothing you can do to win them back.

Comedians talk about stand-up in very hostile terms. If you have a good gig, you 'killed', and if you have a bad gig, you 'died'. It's kill or be killed. Witnessing a death onstage is excruciating. Experiencing it is indescribable. The worst death I ever saw was during my brief stint at Edinburgh University, years before I took to the stage myself. I never knew the comic's name and haven't seen him since. This career path was certainly evident that night, as he performed to near silence. It was a packed audience of about 400, including a gallery. The comedian was fighting for his life, sweating, dry mouth, throwing every joke he could think of at it. No response. People were turning away, chatting among themselves.

Now, I don't know if it was thrown or dropped, but somehow a lit cigarette originating from the gallery landed on the comedian's head. As it burned away atop his full head of hair, the audience started noticing the cigarette and giggling. Unaware of the lit cigarette, the comedian's eyes lit up, too. 'I've cracked them!' he was thinking. He then started to loosen up, moisture flooded back into his throat, the sweat on his brow began to clear, and he confidently launched into more material. Flames started to plume from his head. The giggles now escalated into fully blown laughter. He thought he was Richard Pryor, but looked more like Michael Jackson making a Pepsi commercial.

'You're on fire, mate!' someone shouted from the crowd.

He took this as a compliment.

'Do you like impressions?' he said, feeling like a star.

The audience were now weak from laughter, tears rolling down their student faces as he broke into his 'Michael Crawford', not realizing he was already doing a pretty good 'Guy Fawkes'. It looked for all the world as though this 'dying' comedian might die for real. People were laughing so hard at the situation, they were unable to tell him he was ablaze, and he was so thrilled at the response to his 'ooh Betty' to notice. Eventually, just after he'd commented on the non-existent smoke machine, he ran from the stage screaming. It was a horror story and not for a moment was I thinking, 'That's what I want to do for a living.'

However bulletproof you think your 'set' is, a comic can die onstage at any time. From what I've been told, my dad didn't need to use his 'No Laughs' jokes very often. He opened for the Rolling Stones and lived for a while with Irish comedian Dave Allen, who told my mum years later that my dad was extremely talented. But, unlike myself, I don't think his vocation was to perform, and his move behind the camera began when he devised the comedy panel show *Jokers Wild* for Yorkshire Television. Hosted by Barry Cryer, the format was simple: Barry would give two teams of three comedians a subject to make a joke about. During the joke, a member of the other team could buzz in and finish it for points. It's like *Mock the Week* but with flares, corduroy and more manners. The show was a hit and ran for eight series, regularly featuring Les Dawson, John Cleese (Cheese), Arthur Askey, Michael Aspel and my dad himself.

As indicated by my birth certificate, my dad was primarily involved in the music industry. It was during *Jokers Wild* that he met Clive Dunn and recorded 'Grandad'. He and his partner Alan Hawkshaw (who signs his emails 'Hawk') were writing and recording songs. I met Alan when I was about thirteen. He's a hilarious character. My dad, my sister and I went to his enormous house in Radlett, Hertfordshire. Music had been good to the Hawk, one piece of music in particular. He wrote a thirty-second tune that made him a fortune. Can you guess it?

Here's a clue . . . It's exactly thirty seconds long.

Here's another . . . Du-du . . . Du-du . . . De-de-dede . . . Boom!

Yes, that's right, *Countdown*.

(I actually met Carol Vorderman once in a lift. I got in and she was standing at the numbers and asked me, 'What floor?' If I couldn't make a joke in these circumstances, I'm in the wrong business. 'One from the top and four from anywhere else, please, Carol.')

34

Those thirty seconds netted the Hawk a fortune. His house had its own recording studio, swimming pool, snooker room. He gets paid every time it's played, that's every weekday at about 4.56 p.m. He actually gets paid by the second, so the longer it takes for people to guess the conundrum, the more money he makes. You can imagine him in the eighties, turning on the telly at 4.55 p.m., hoping the contestants can't decipher the conundrum so that he can afford a better holiday.

Countdown aficionados (judging by the number of adverts they have for Tena Lady in the break, *Countdown* is mainly watched by women who pee in their pants) will know that if the contestant buzzes in to guess the conundrum, the clock stops. If they correctly identify the jumbled-up nine-letter word, the game is over. However, if they get it wrong, the clock restarts, which means more money for Alan. You can only imagine the excitement in the Hawk household, whooping and cheering when they guess incorrectly, wild applause, back-slapping and champagne corks popping when the tune reaches its 'De-de-de-de . . . Boom' climax.

My sister and I loved Alan as soon as we met him. He was a charming and personable man. Within moments of our arriving, he sat at his grand piano and dramatically played various TV themes he had written that we might recognize, including the original *Grange Hill*. It's wonderful to see someone so proud of their work, and I have to say his rendition of *Countdown* was one of the most moving thirty seconds of my life. We drove for a pub lunch in his new Japanese sports car, in which he played all his own music, announcing, 'I only ever listen to my own music in the car.'

As the pub was about ten minutes away, I remember thinking, 'I'm glad he has an extensive canon of work – otherwise we'd have to listen to *Countdown* twenty times back to back.'

So Alan and my dad were writing music and producing records in the sixties and seventies. In 1975, my father found a song and was looking for a singer. This is basically record producing in its purest form. He held auditions in his small office off Trafalgar Square, and in walked my mum, a bleached-blonde beauty young enough to be his daughter. 'If you can sing half as good as you look, we're going to be rich,' observed my dad.

She couldn't. Her audition was appalling. If she was on *The X-Factor*, Louis would have said through his giggles, 'I'm sorry, you look great, but I don't think singing is for you'; Dannii would have said, silently seething over how gorgeous Cheryl looks, 'It was a bit out of tune'; Cheryl would have diplomatically said, 'I think you're luverly, but I think you're a bit out of your depth singing, sorry, luv'; and Simon would have said, 'I give up', and then walked off set, immediately cancelling *The X-Factor*, *American Idol* and *Britain's Got Talent*, retiring from showbusiness to become a recluse with nobody knowing his whereabouts, apart from Sinitta.

My father's reaction was less drastic. One thing led to another and before you knew it, I was peeing on the doctor in a hospital in Merton in 1976, which probably came as a relief to the doctor as much as me due to the Sahara-like temperatures.

4

When my mum fell pregnant (an odd expression: 'Wow, you're pregnant, what happened?' 'I fell . . . on top of that man') with my sister Lucy, we moved in search of more space. We found it in a ground floor flat in leafy Hampstead. I know what you're thinking – Kensington? Hampstead? La-di-da. I know. There's no denying I had a pretty decent start. This is primarily due to my grandma ('Helloo, daaarling') marrying Jim, the wealthy Scrabble-losing stockbroker.

I can only imagine my father's face when he found out this beautiful nineteen-year-old had rich parents too. And you can only imagine my grandma and Jim's faces when they found out their daughter was marrying a thirty-seven-year-old Canadian comedian who went by several different names and whose greatest success was producing Clive Dunn's 'Grandad'. The relationship between my dad and grandparents was uneasy, to say the least. My mother recalls how on their first meeting my dad addressed the thorny issue of their wealth, saying, 'I'm a bit worried about your money.'

To which my grandmother replied, 'Don't vorry about it, you're not gettiing it.'

Relations certainly weren't improved when my dad sold their holiday home in Malta, which Grandma and Jim had put in my mother's name for tax reasons. I tried to talk him out of it, but my vocabulary was limited to 'Ma', 'Da' and 'Shums' (my word for 'shoes'). I threw up on his shoulder, but it had little impact. The Maltese house was sold, and the Hampstead flat bought with the proceeds.

My mother was expecting her second child. I wasn't. I thought she'd let herself go. I didn't know she was about to give birth to a rival. I was the centre of attention at home. I was used to having everything my own way. I was the main man. Then one day my mum suddenly lost a tremendous amount of weight and there was this baby stealing my limelight. 'Isn't she beautiful?', 'Can I hold her?', 'Look at those little hands', 'Adorable', gushed friends and relatives.

'Michael, do you want to say hello to your new little sister?' my dad asked.

'Keep that little bitch away from me,' I tried to say, although all that came out was, 'Ma, Da, Shums.'

It was a shock to have competition at home, but I had to see the positives of having a sibling and a growing family. Unfortunately, I couldn't and decided to try to kill my sister instead. According to my mother, up until Lucy was about six months old, I made several attempts on her life. Much like a Mafia hit, I would win her and my parents' trust before striking. I would gently stroke her cheek, before trying to suffocate her with her own frilly booties. I would sweetly comb her hair, and then bash her in the temple with the brush. I poisoned her rusks with red berries I found in the garden and tried to drown her so many times that we had to take separate baths.

I'm pleased to say I finally accepted my sister and together we got on with the business of growing up in the eighties. But, in truth, there was another child in the house. Our mum. To give you an idea of the age gap, my mum once sprained her ankle and my father rushed her to Casualty, where the doctor said, 'If you would like to just pop your leg up on Daddy's knee.' This pissed my dad off so much he sent my mum straight to bed without a story.

In America, she would only just have been allowed to drink alcohol, but here she was raising two kids and learning on the job. It's a job she did wonderfully well, with only the occasional hitch. For example, normally an adult would tell the kids to buckle up in the car, but nobody wore a seatbelt in my mum's mustard-coloured Ford Capri. My sister and I would just bounce around in the back, occasionally clinging on to the front seats for survival. And remember, there were no speed bumps in those days. By the end of a journey, I would often end up in the front and my sister on the ledge in front of the back window with Bronski Beat playing at full volume.

Family cars containing young kids will always be untidy.

However, this is usually confined to the back. Not my mum's Capri. The Capri was filthy in both the children's area and my mum's area. Strewn all over the front of the car would be crisp packets, bits of old chewing gum, magazines (yes, she would read at the traffic lights), Coke cans, old lipsticks and cassettes with unwound tape hanging out of them.

Occasionally my mother would clean the car, by throwing things out of the window, in traffic. Once she threw so much litter out of the car at rush hour on the Finchley Road that my sister and I sat open-mouthed in amazement in the back. Literally, she chucked about four magazines into the street while Kajagoogoo blared out of her Blaupunkt stereo. Moments later somebody got out of their car, picked up my mum's discarded debris, and threw it back into our car. Unperturbed, my mum promptly threw it out again. This continued all the way between St John's Wood and Hampstead.

Once, when we went shopping on Hampstead High Street, my mother loaded the boot with groceries, put me in the back seat and drove off. A few miles later, she started to get a nagging feeling she'd forgotten something. PG Tips? Shake n' Vac? Culture Club's 'Do You Really Want to Hurt Me?' on 7-inch vinyl from Our Price? No, my sister Lucy, who was still in her pram on the pavement fifteen minutes later when we returned. 'Why didn't you say anything?' my mother screamed, blaming me.

'Hey, I've been trying to kill that bitch for months,' I said, although this came out as 'Ma, Da, Shums.'

After I moved to Tanta in Egypt with my Lebanese Catholic parents Joseph and Abia ... (Oh no, I've slipped back into Omar Sharif's autobiography. What's wrong with me?)

In my teens, I fell ill (nothing serious, don't worry) and checked in at the doctor's surgery reception in Hendon. The receptionist handed me my medical notes and said, 'Please give these to the doctor, and you're not allowed to look at them.'

'Of course not,' I lied.

Moments later, out of sight, I had a flick through my little malady memoirs. I got quite nostalgic about my 'pain in the abdominal area' of March 1987, my 'blurred vision' of May 1985 and my 'soreness in left ear' of November 1983. What surprised me, however, were the first few entries. 'Michael not talking. Parents worried.' 'Michael still not talking, just grunting. Parents increasingly concerned.' 'Michael only saying a few words. Worrying rate of development. Should be monitored. Only says "Ma", "Da" and "Shums".' I was shocked to find out that my early medical history was remarkably similar to Forrest Gump's. Apparently my sister spoke before me despite being two years younger. Her first words were 'Is Michael retarded?'

My younger son, Oscar, is nearly two and only has one word, 'hoover', which he calls 'hooba'. Out of all the things in the world, why 'hoover'? My oldest, Lucas, who is four and a half – his first word was 'car'. I have no idea why, but I suppose you've got to start somewhere. Maybe they'll go into business together one day and run 'McIntyre Brothers', a car valeting service.

So my memories really start to kick in at our Hampstead flat, which I remember to be quite dimly lit. Maybe at my parents' height this was 'mood lighting', but from where my sister and I were crawling, it was just dark. The flat was in a big old Edwardian building that also contained three other flats.

The room I remember most is the living room. This is odd, because it's the only room that my sister and I were strictly forbidden to enter. I became obsessed with the living room, presumably because it was out of bounds. The living room was darker than the rest of the house, with dark green sofas and lots of plants. Because I was only two foot tall, to me it was like an indoor night jungle with soft furnishings. 'Don't go in there, that's Mummy and Daddy's special room.' Special room? What goes on in that mini-Jurassic Park of theirs?

My wife and I do the same today with our kids. We don't let them in the living room because it's our special room that we want to keep nice. I'm sure many people reading this can relate to keeping the front room child-free. But if I'm honest, my wife and I never go in there, and nor did my parents ever go in theirs. Let's face it, the country is filled with homes, each with an immaculate room that nobody goes in. We buy and rent accommodation and don't use all of it. The only time we've used our living room, and the only time I remember using the living room in my childhood Hampstead flat, was on Christmas Day. It's a room reserved for one day of the year. This is OK if you live in a mansion, but this was a cramped flat. It made no sense to me as I toddled around that we'd cordoned off part of it for just one day of the year.

One dinnertime, while enjoying a beef broth vegetable medley compote, I addressed my parents: 'This living room situation is a joke. Why don't you sub-let it? I was chatting to a girl at playgroup, and she says her parents do the same thing. Maybe we could solve the homeless problem if we, as a nation, open up our unused front rooms? We'd have to kick them out on Christmas Day, but the rest of the year would be good for them. And that's another thing. If it's just a "Christmas room", why don't you leave the Christmas tree and decorations up all year? And why have you got so many plants in such a dark room, have you never heard of photosynthesis? What kind of people are you?'

Unfortunately, my rant sounded more like an episode of *Pingu*, and my dad just muttered, 'We should go back to the doctor, his speech isn't improving at all.'

My parents' actual room was not out of bounds. Every morning my sister and I would climb into our parents' bed. I would always go on our dad's side and

Lucy would always go on our mum's side. I don't know why it was always this way round. All I know is that, with all due respect to my father, I got the bum draw, almost literally. We must have been very young at this time; in fact this might rival Poo-gate as my earliest memory. I love cuddling my two boys but seldom wonder what the experience might be like for them. They are little, soft and wonderful. I am not.

Well, I vividly recall these early-morning cuddles with my dad. Not only was he a big naked hairy man, but his mouth was about the size of my little head. I will never forget his hot cigarettey breath blasting into my tiny face. At regular intervals, my hair would be blown horizontal as I would try to avoid it, like Keanu Reeves avoiding bullets in the *Matrix* trilogy.

Morning breath (something I have discussed at length in stand-up) is bad enough – cigarettes certainly don't improve things. Occasionally my father would be sipping coffee in bed. The combination of morning breath, cigarette breath and coffee breath became almost lethal. I think he was one garlic clove away from actually killing me. I would peek over to the other side, where Lucy and my mother were enjoying day-beginning cuddles and then return to my father's life-threatening monster breath blowing a gale into my face. Come to think of it, maybe this is what was affecting my vocal cords. Maybe my morning dad cuddles also shaped the way I look. Nowadays I always look a bit windswept and squinting, which is exactly how I would have looked in the eye of his breath-storm.

My dad was a heavy smoker. Outside of his wives and children, the two great loves of his life were Marlboro and Camel. He began smoking as a twelve-year-old in Montreal when, believe it or not, smoking was encouraged for health reasons. Then, your 'five a day' referred to cigarettes. It was as if he smoked every minute of the day. Remember in those days there were no restrictions on smoking. So he'd be smoking in restaurants, on aeroplanes, in cinemas, on the bus, on the Tube. He was smoking when he said his marriage vows, he smoked while sleeping and when he swam underwater. My dad never managed to quit.

I myself started smoking as a teenager and smoked about a pack of Marlboro Lights a day until my mid-twenties. Giving up was one of the biggest achievements of my life. I read Allen Carr's book *How to Stop Smoking* and would recommend it to anybody trying to kick the filthy habit. In fact, I have recommended it many times, including to a very sweet, chain-smoking former tour manager of mine who then accidentally read Alan Carr's *Look Who It Is!*, the 2008 autobiography by everyone's favourite camp comedian. He then bizarrely reported, 'I read that Alan Carr book you told me about. I thought it was hilarious and yes, I have been smoking less, thank you.'

Apart from my parents' room and the living room, the

rest of our Hampstead flat is a bit of a blur. Strangely, comedy was already in the building as living in the flat above was the comedy writer John Junkin, who appeared with the Beatles in the film *A Hard Day's Night*. I don't ever remember him upright. He was always sitting, in fact almost lying, in his chair, and he seemed to have most of his life around his neck. His glasses were on a cord hanging around his neck, as were his lighter and a bottle opener. I think he might have also had a compass and maybe a medal for the longest time sat in one chair. Even as a toddler who could only grunt I thought, 'That's odd.' The other bizarre thing in the Junkin household was the astonishing amount of Lucozade. This family was addicted to Lucozade. The whole flat had a sort of orange glow, like David Dickinson's bathroom.

John was married to Jenny. Jenny and my mother became the best of friends almost immediately, chatting to each other, from their respective flats, through make-shift telephones made of plastic cups and string. My mother's name was Kati, pronounced 'Cottee' (I can't believe I haven't mentioned this before), but Jenny called her 'Coke', a nickname that stuck for some time. Looking back, it seems the Junkins were really into fizzy drinks, what with the Lucozade everywhere and calling my mum 'Coke'. When Jenny fell on John, she too became pregnant and had a child called Annabelle, which was disappointing as my sister and I had a side bet she would be called 7-Up or Dr Pepper.

Soon after we moved into our dimly lit Hampstead flat underneath the Junkins' Lucozade-glowing abode, my dad's career in comedy began in earnest. Barry Cryer was hired to write for a zany and wildly talented radio DJ, Kenny Everett. Kenny was moving to television with *The Kenny Everett Video Show* on Thames TV. Barry, who had worked with my dad on *Jokers Wild*, brought him in to help with a segment of the show. The three of them hit it off immediately, and to such an extent that my dad was hired for the whole series. The chemistry between Kenny, Barry and my dad was perfect, and they laughed their way through series after series of a show that was getting up to 20 million viewers.

In those days there were only three channels, BBC1, BBC2 and ITV. It must be impossible for teenagers, reading this book on their iPad, to fathom such a thing. It wasn't really so bad. The only real difference is that in 1980 someone would ask, 'What's on TV tonight?' and ten seconds later the reply would be 'Nothing', whereas in 2010 when someone asks, 'What's on TV tonight?' it takes half an hour before somebody says, 'Nothing.'

TV was so much simpler then. Today I can hardly keep up with technology. I've just got HD; now I'm told it's all about 3D. 3D technology is truly amazing, and soon we will get to experience it in our own homes. The problem I have is that, sure it's amazing if you're watching *Avatar*. I've seen *Avatar*. It's unbelievable – you feel like you can reach out and touch the Na'vi characters and are surrounded by the landscape of Pandora, and you can practically smell it. But do we really want to be sitting at home watching TV and feeling like we can reach out and touch Jeremy Kyle? I don't want to feel surrounded by the Loose Women, and I certainly don't want to feel I can practically smell Alan Titchmarsh.

For parents, TV is a salvation. It's well-earned time off. 'Sit down and watch this, kids, while I briefly return to a life I left behind.' My four-year-old, Lucas, even has his own mini-DVD player, so while Oscar's watching *Teletubbies*, he'll be watching *Finding Nemo* on his portable. (When school was cancelled for a week during the snow, I think he watched every U and PG film ever made. He had to start on the 12s and 15s. When the snow finally melted, he was half-way through *Carlito's Way*.)

When I was a kid, my sister and I watched our fair share of telly. 'Don't sit too close or your eyes will go square,' our mum would say before getting back to her colouring in. (The 'eyes going square' risk fascinated me, as did the 'if you sneeze with your eyes open, your eyes will pop out' claim. I spent countless hours trying to get my sister to sneeze while sitting too close to the TV, hoping her square eyes would pop out.)

We watched all the classics that will hit readers of a certain age with nostalgia. My favourites were *Sesame Street*, *The Perils of Penelope Pitstop*, *Battle of the Planets* and *Buck Rogers*. I could tolerate *Rainbow* but was not a fan of *Playschool* or *Blue Peter*; I found the presenters really patronizing. I know they were talking to children, but I just thought they were acting weird. The much-loved Floella Benjamin, for example, I couldn't stand her. She was just way too over the top for me (and her first name sounded like a vaccine). I preferred the company of Big Bird, the Cookie Monster, Mr Snuffleupagus, and Bert and Ernie.

It was years later when it struck me that Bert and Ernie must be gay. 'Good night, Bert', 'Good night, Ernie' – they were sleeping in the same bed. I know this may come as a Michael Barrymore/George Michael/ Rock Hudson-scale shock to some, but the evidence is there. They were flatmates. Flatmates would normally have their own room or at least have their own bed – if not, then it's got to be a 'head to toe' sleeping arrangement. Flatmates in the same bed sleeping head-to-head? Gay.

We only had a television in our parents' room, and Lucy and I would sit on the floor in front of their bed. Occasionally, we would watch TV as a family. The main event was always *The Kenny Everett Show* because it was 'Daddy's show'. *The Kenny Everett Show* was famed for the rule-breaking sound of the crew laughing at the sketches rather than canned laughs or the laughs of a live studio audience. My dad had the biggest booming laugh. He would constantly be laughing uproariously. So the laughter on *The Kenny Everett Show* was mainly my dad, which would have a twofold effect when we watched the show at home. He would be laughing on the TV and laughing behind me in his bed. I could barely hear the jokes.

Another evening I recall when we watched TV as a family was the launch of Channel Four in 1982. At last we would be getting a fourth channel. We gathered in my parents' bedroom for what was a spectacular anti-climax. *Countdown*. I think the whole nation felt let down and immediately went back to the BBC and ITV, apart from Alan Hawkshaw, who went shopping.

People look back fondly at a time with so few channels because the nation was all watching pretty much the same thing. We therefore had more in common with each other, leading to what the Americans call 'water-cooler moments'. This is when people discuss the previous night's television at the water-cooler. This expression has crept into our nation's lexicon (I know, 'lexicon', quite a fancy word for me). I think 'water-cooler moments' are purely an American thing, and the expression has no place over here. British people don't speak to each other anywhere, let alone at water-coolers. The only thing a British person has said to another British person at the water-cooler is 'There's no more water' or 'We need more cups' or 'Sorry'.

I do think, though, that the multi-channels of today are great for kids. There are countless kids' channels that are on twenty-four hours a day. If you have kids (or just enjoy unchallenging TV), it doesn't matter what time it is, you can turn on the telly and watch *Ben 10* or *Bob the Builder*. Whereas in the early eighties, my sister and I could only watch television intended for us at certain times, which led to us watching a lot of TV that wasn't intended for us. I remember watching a lot of snooker on BBC2. My mother was forever trying to find Ray Reardon and Cliff Thorburn figures in toy shops. The film *The Towering Inferno* was on seemingly every day during the 1980s. It was on more than the weather forecast. It would be the news, *The Towering Inferno*, then the weather. Every time I turned the TV on, Robert Wagner was hanging out of a burning building. It was repeated so many times, I think I once watched it back to back.

It was during my childhood TV viewing that I found out I was heterosexual. I can actually pinpoint the moment. It was in 1983, so I was seven years old and watching Billy Joel's 'Uptown Girl' video featuring the model Christie Brinkley. She was gorgeous. I felt peculiar. I revisited those feelings a few times pre-puberty, and approximately every seven seconds post-puberty. Lynda Carter's *Wonder Woman* was a favourite, as was golden-bikini-clad Princess Leia, obviously, and there was a scene in *Flash Gordon* (the camp one with music by Queen – 'Flash, Aaaaa!') where Princess Aura is being whipped that I rewound so many time the video tape broke – as did the video player and the television. (I've just looked the clip up on YouTube. Tremendous.)

I got carried away a bit there with eighties television – back to the story. So there I was with my vocabulary of three words watching *The Towering Inferno*, toddling around our little Hampstead flat, keeping out of the living room, with my baby sister who I had made feel a bit like Sarah Connor from *The Terminator*. I was being raised by my mum, who looked more suited to Wham!'s 'Club Tropicana' video, and by my chain-smoking, booming-laughing, *Kenny Everett Show*-writing dad.

My family. All together. But not for long.

That's a very dramatic end to quite a light chapter. It's designed to make you read on.

5

A child's job is relatively simple. At breakfast-time your goal is to eat the sweetest option available, Frosties, Ricicles, Sugar Puffs, or ideally just a bowl of sugar with a sprinkle of sugar. If you're leaving the house, you want to leave it until the last possible minute when your mother reaches a certain decibel of helplessness. Then you must lose one shoe – 'For Chrissake, where's your other shoe?' – and avoid wearing a coat regardless of the temperature: 'I don't wunna wear a coat.' When in the road, your goal is to avoid handholding and to explore the city on your own. Splashing in the bath is fun, but everything else in the bathroom is unnecessary. You never want to brush your teeth, and if you're a boy having your hair washed, you will scream like a girl, and if you're a girl, you will just scream.

At mealtimes, you will find one food that you like (chicken nuggets, pasta) and stick to it. Despite your parents' claim that vegetables are good for you, you and other kids know the truth. They are deadly and to be avoided at all costs; the only things good for you are sweets, chocolate and ice cream. 'Bedtime' is a concept created by adults, but in actual fact does not exist. There is no time of bed. Sleep is not needed. Do everything you can to delay getting into bed. When finally in bed being read a story, always aim for one more story than has been agreed. Shouting 'One more!' usually does the trick.

As a parent your job is to threaten your children, often with death, so they do what you want. 'If you don't wear a coat, you will die of pneumonia', 'If you don't hold my hand, a car will hit you and kill you', 'If you don't brush your teeth, they will rot and fall out, then you can't eat and you will die', 'If you don't wash your hair, you will get worms living in it that will eat into your head and kill you', 'If you don't eat your vegetables, your bones will crumble and you will die', 'If you don't go to bed now, I will strangle you to death.'

The problem is that kids don't really believe their parents' threats. Personally, I didn't listen to my mum because she wasn't wearing a coat, ate Frosties and screamed when my father washed her hair. I think they should have broadcast a fake *Newsround* every day with John Craven saying things like, 'Today, previously healthy Jamie Dunn, aged five and a half, from Milton Keynes, died instantly from pneumonia after leaving the house without his coat. Jamie's mother said, "I warned him, but he just didn't listen." Today's weather will be warm, but nothing like 1976. Stay tuned for *The Towering Inferno.*'

My sister and I would not only be battling our mum

for more sweets and toys, but also be in competition with each other for various childhood perks.

'I want to go first.'

'No, I want to go first.'

'Let your sister have a bite.'

'No, it's mine.'

'I want the window seat.'

'No, I want the window seat.'

'I want to sit in the front.'

'No, I want to sit in the front.'

Which is why it came as a surprise when we got bunk beds, and I said, 'I want the top bunk' and my sister answered, 'OK.'

'No, I want the top bunk,' I replied automatically.

'I don't want it,' reiterated my sister.

I couldn't believe this. The top bunk is where it's at. Elevated sleeping is the Holy Grail of child slumber. I can see our room, indeed the world, from a new perspective from up there, like the students in *Dead Poets Society* standing on their desks. 'Are you sure, Lucy?'

'Yes, Michael, I don't want to sleep on the top bunk.' *Carpe diem*, I'm taking it. That night our dad read us a story, kissed us goodnight and dimmed the light, leaving us just enough illumination not to be scared.

'Lucy?' I said from my upper berth.

'What? Don't interrupt me, I'm drifting off to sleep,' came the reply from beneath. Like all little girls, she was articulate and advanced beyond her years.

'Why didn't you want the top bunk?'

'Because the ceiling is going to fall down in this room, and it's safer down here,' she answered factually.

'No it isn't,' I said.

'Do you see that crack in the ceiling? That will worsen and the ceiling will fall,' she insisted.

'Don't be stupid,' I said, before losing consciousness.

Every night, without fail, my sister would go to bed muttering about how the ceiling was going to cave in. I thought she was mad. And then, one day, the ceiling fell in. I remember my dad coming home from work with a smile on his face, which soon disappeared when he saw my mum and me standing in the front porch in tears with bits of ceiling in our hair. We weren't hurt, although I received a glancing blow from one of the Junkins' Lucozade bottles. (Luckily, it was a 125ml, and in the days before the '25% Extra Free'.)

Lucy was at the kitchen table combing the hair of a My Little Pony, rocking backwards and forwards, saying, 'I told you', looking like a character from a Japanese horror movie. For a while after her disaster prophecy, I was quite fearful of Lucy, especially when she became best friends with Annabelle Junkin from upstairs. Annabelle had fiery red hair and fair skin. Lucy and Annabelle standing together at the end of a corridor looked like a scene from Stanley Kubrick's *The Shining*. I would spend days hiding behind plants in the out-of-bounds living room. Was my baby sister some kind of modern-day Nostradamus? Soon we settled back into a relationship typical of siblings with a two-year age gap. We fought with each other and loved each other. We slept in the same room, had baths with each other, ate with each other and went to pre-school together.

My pre-school, Stepping Stones, the scene of the Poo-gate incident that scarred me for life, was a stone's throw from our Hampstead flat. Mum would drop us off in her Capri every morning, although sometimes she let me drive. Lucy would go to her class and I to mine. I certainly didn't enjoy it there, but what I hated more than anything else in my life, then or since, was school lunch.

Still to this day I cannot eat peas because of the memory of the Stepping Stones peas. They made me feel sick to my stomach. Just the smell of peas now and I am catapulted back in my mind to those horror school lunches when I was five years old. Sitting at long tables, with the white noise of children chatting and cutlery clattering, I would stare at my 'lunch', intermittently retching. The teachers would prowl up and down the tables like Dementors from *Harry Potter*, making sure you ate all your food. There was categorically no way I was going to put those peas in my mouth. So I would take a handful of them and, when the teacher wasn't looking, throw them on the floor under the table. I got away with it. Every day, if I didn't like something, I would subtly throw it on the floor. Some days I would just tip up the whole plate.

I don't really understand why I was being made to eat all my food when it was so disgusting. This was a private school; my grandmother ('Heelooo, daarling') was paying good money for this. The teacher should come over to my table and say, 'Is everything all right with the food, sir?'

I would reply, 'No, the peas are making me vomit.' Then he would apologize profusely, immediately remove my plate and take some money off the school fees as a goodwill gesture.

But we had to finish our revolting food or be forced to. So I took drastic measures, and, to be honest, I thought I was a genius to be getting away with it. However, it transpired that the teachers were fully aware of my devious dumping. In fact, unbeknownst to me, they were watching me in the wings and giggling as I tried to get rid of my peas, like Steve McQueen discarding earth in *The Great Escape*. Everyone had been watching and laughing, even the kids. It was soul-destroying. The teachers had a word with my mum, and soon peas were off the menu, and have been ever since.

While I was throwing peas on the floor, my mum was throwing magazines out of her car window and Lucy was predicting domestic disasters, my dad's career continued to blossom. *The Kenny Everett Show* moved to BBC1 on Thursday nights after *Top of the Pops*. The nation was in love with 'cuddly Ken' and our life was becoming quite glamorous. Kenny was just about the most famous man in the country. Many readers will remember, but for younger readers who don't, Kenny Everett was a sensation. It's difficult to think of the equivalent today. His show was being watched by more people than watch *The X-Factor*. He was hysterically funny and loveable. Kenny and my dad clicked creatively, but Kenny and my mum clicked in every other way. My mum, 'Coke', became quite the fag hag. They became the best of friends. In fact, I remember my mum together with Kenny more than I remember my mum together with my dad.

The weekly shop is probably the least glamorous part of life. Not for my mum. The nation's favourite funnyman, Kenny Everett, would join her in Waitrose, Temple Fortune. Kenny in his beige bomber jacket with fluffy collar and my blonde mum in her dungarees, would pick up a bottle of champagne each from 'Aisle 12, Alcohol and Beverages', then return to 'Aisle 1, Fruit and Vegetables', pop open their bottles of bubby and giggle their way round the supermarket. Kenny was such a megastar he could do as he pleased. The Waitrose staff loved it. Crowds of onlookers would gather outside as word spread on the normally sleepy suburban high street. Kenny would be cracking jokes about detergents and biscuits between signing autographs and swigging Bollinger, while my mum would be laughing hysterically, sometimes from inside the trolley.

After the shopping was done – 'Come on, Coke, I'm

ravenous' – it would be off to La Sorpresa in Hampstead for lunch, where the Italian waiters welcomed them with open arms.

'Mr Kenny, Miss Coca-Cola, hello, come have seat, favourite table.'

In they would stumble. Kenny was in the closet at this time, so everyone thought they were a couple. My mum would often be referred to as 'mystery blonde' in the tabloids. There was so much goodwill towards Kenny (he once knocked over a cyclist in his BMW who proceeded to ask for an autograph) that lunch was usually on the house. Either they would frame the cheque or just refuse payment. Once Kenny didn't have a pen and wrote the cheque using toothpaste they'd just bought from Waitrose. 'You're so funny, Mr Kenny.'

He wouldn't just eat for free, but also take whatever he fancied from the restaurant. 'Do you like this vase, Coke?'

'I love it,' giggled my mother. 'I quite like that ashtray, too.' They would leave the restaurant with most of the tableware (and once a lamp) with the full blessing of the Italian owner, who would be laughing and applauding his celebrity guest as Kenny and my mum walked out with nearly enough furnishings to open their own Italian restaurant.

After lunch they would pick up Lucy and me from school. You can only imagine the looks on the other conservative parents' faces when my mum walked through the school gates in fits of laughter on Kenny Everett's arm. As the schoolchildren came out, Kenny would guess their future professions: 'Accountant', 'Wrestler', 'Osteopath', 'Dictator'. The kids themselves went nuts with excitement. When the future accountant, wrestler, osteopath and dictator saw Kenny, it was bedlam. The day after the first time Kenny collected me from school, my popularity rocketed.

'Is Kenny Everett your dad?', 'Is Kenny Everett your dad?' I must have been asked a hundred times by everyone from my friends to the teachers, dinner ladies and, coolest of all, the big boys. This was a crunch moment for me. I'd gone from pea-dropping freak to potentially the most popular boy in school, and it seemed to hinge on my response. 'Is Kenny Everett your dad?'

I paused, thinking of my real dad, who I loved and was my hero. 'Yes, Kenny Everett is my dad,' I said. I was the most popular kid in school.

My popularity lasted a term and a half until the fathers' race at sports day. I don't think there has been as much excitement surrounding a hundred-metre dash since Jesse Owens claimed Gold in the 1936 Berlin Olympics. I was terrified about my lie being revealed. My dad looks nothing like Kenny Everett. On the morning of sports day, I tried to convince my father not to attend, but he was breathing hot coffee, cigarettey morning breath into my face at the time, which I think muffled my request. The crowd was enormous, every pupil and parent focusing on the starting line. Other events occurring elsewhere on the sports field were completely ignored as child competitors looked confused as to why their parents hadn't shown up to cheer them on.

'Where is he? Where is he?' murmured sections of the crowd. Some parents had dressed up as their favourite *Kenny Everett Show* characters; I saw three Sid Snots and a Cupid Stunt. I couldn't bear to watch. When my dad was introduced there was a gasp from the crowd. Not before or since has an athletics crowd been so disappointed (Ben Johnson's 1988 cheating doesn't come close). The Cupid Stunt ripped off his wig and stormed off to his car, still in his fake tits.

'Kenny Everett's not your dad', 'Kenny Everett's not your dad', 'You're a liar', 'Liar', said everyone from my friends and the teachers, to the dinner ladies and, worst of all, the big boys. I was the least popular kid in school.

Oh, and I should also mention my dad came last in the race, and in the wheelbarrow race I fell and landed head-first on a fake egg, from the earlier egg-and-spoon race, which gouged my eye. All in all, a terrible day.

This wasn't the only time I lied as a child. There is one lie that I have carried with me until this very moment, in this very book. In the summer holidays after my disastrous sports day, we went on holiday to Florida. We stayed at the Hilton Fontainebleau, an enormous hotel seen on the opening credits of *Miami*

Vice with Don Johnson. Lucy and I loved it there. There was a waterfall and waterslide into the pool. My father got into a row with the manager at breakfast because a pot of coffee cost differing amounts depending on how many people were drinking it, even though it was the same sized pot. So if ten people had a sip each, it cost ten times the amount of one person drinking the whole pot. It makes me angry just thinking about it. Anyway, that's not why I'm telling you this.

During our stay a major motion picture was being filmed at the hotel, resulting in part of the pool being closed for a few days. The film was the cult classic *Scarface* starring Al Pacino. The poster has adorned the walls of just about every teenage boy's bedroom of the past twenty-five years. There's a scene where the camera pans across the beach, and I claimed that I was in the shot for a split second. Everybody believed me. I have been gaining credibility over my *Scarface* appearance ever since. People don't question it – they just say, 'Wow, cool, you were in *Scarface*, that's awesome.' I wasn't. I lied.

Kenny and my mum weren't just spending days together; they were partying into the night, too. My dad was literally from a different generation to my mum, so after a hard day's writing or filming, he just wanted a good meal, a hot bath and a thousand Marlboros. The problem was his wife was in her early twenties and wanted to party. It's a bit like getting a Labrador; they're really cute and blonde but a lot of work. 'Coke' had devoted much of her youth to motherhood. You just don't see a lot of pregnant or breastfeeding women in nightclubs. But now the kids had been weaned and she wanted to go out with her new girlfriend, Kenny Everett. My dad was happy, it meant my mum could burn some of her youthful energy in the company of homosexuals who were no threat to him.

So my mum would dance the night away at nightclubs such as Heaven and Stringfellows. In fact, for years there was a photo of them together adorning a wall inside Stringfellows. My dad would catch up on their exploits in the tabloids the next morning. Kenny would make up a different name for my mum every time they were papped coming out of a club; my favourite was 'Melody Bubbles'. Heaven is, and was, London's largest and most renowned gay club. Melody Bubbles would be the only girl in there, dancing the night away with just about every gay man from the 1980s, including Freddie Mercury, Boy George and *Sesame Street*'s Bert and Ernie.

Today, there is a comedy club that uses Heaven nightclub between 8 p.m. and 11 p.m., before it is open to gentlemen of a certain persuasion. I've performed there many times; it's actually a great space for comedy. On leaving the venue, I've seen the gay men queuing for entry to the club. Security seems to be quite an issue. They have an airport-style metal-detecting security arch outside. I don't know if they are worried about weapons or drugs or if it is some kind of 'gaydar' machine that beeps if you're not gay.

Next to the detector was a gentleman frisker who looked like Jean-Claude Van Damme in a muscle vest and tight white jeans. It seemed obvious that the queue would much rather be frisked than not. There was huge disappointment when there was no beep. I saw one man make his own beeping sound and then jump into the arms of the frisker. People were holding whatever metal they could get their hands on to guarantee the detector sounded. One guy wasn't leaving anything to chance and had dressed as a knight.

The presence of Kenny and his television show dominated my early years. I visited the TV studio several times and watching the show was the highlight of the week. There would be various props, bits of wardrobe, posters and VHSs from the show knocking around our Hampstead flat. In among them were these postcards with an image of big red smiling sexy lips on them. I don't remember what the reference was, perhaps something to do with Hot Gossip, the Arlene Phillips-choreographed dancers who appeared on the show. I was very familiar with these cards being used for scribbles around our home, shopping lists, phone messages, that kind of thing.

After days of having a wobbly tooth, the landmark occasion of my first tooth falling out was approaching. Your teeth falling out is grim, it's literally like a bad dream, but the carrot was, of course, the Tooth Fairy. When my tooth finally freed itself from my mouth, I was to leave it under my pillow, whereupon a fairy would, in effect, buy it from me. The going rate in 1982 was a pound. Strangely, I think it still is a pound. The Tooth Fairy has obviously never heard of inflation. In fact if milk tooth prices rose in line with, say, house prices, by 2007 the price would have reached £14 (although now it would have dropped to about £12.50). What I never understood about the Tooth Fairy is, what exactly is she doing with these teeth she's collecting? She must have millions of children's milk teeth. Sick. And where does she get the money from? I bet MI5 have a file on her.

Anyway, my tooth finally fell out and I placed it under my pillow. In the morning I was thrilled to find a crisp £1 note under my pillow and something else unexpected. The Tooth Fairy had also left a calling card. It was a card with a photo of a set of glistening perfect white teeth. I immediately recognized this card to be one of the many identical cards from *The Kenny Everett Show* that were scattered all over our flat. I was confused. Why would the Tooth Fairy have one? Could . . . my mum . . . be . . . the . . . Tooth Fairy? I ran into my mum's bedroom. 'Mum, are you the Tooth Fairy?' I enquired.

'Why would you say that, darling?' she replied convincingly.

'Because there was one of these cards under my pillow

and even though it had an image of teeth, which one would associate with the Tooth Fairy, I know these are cards from Daddy's show.'

It was at this point my mother cracked under surprisingly little pressure and gave up all her parenting secrets in one of the most shocking and devastating moments of my life. 'You've got me, you worked it out,' she confessed. 'I am the Tooth Fairy and the Easter Bunny and Father Christmas, don't tell your sister.' Bang, bang, bang. Three in one go.

I can't imagine that in the history of parenting a mother has ever delivered such damaging revelations in such quick succession. I may have been on to the Tooth Fairy, but not for a second had I doubted the authenticity of the Easter Bunny and certainly not Father Christmas. I was mute for three whole days. My parents and all parents for that matter are liars. Well, I wasn't going to be part of their deceit, so I told my sister. Lucy said she already knew and was humouring our parents. Then she said, 'Planes will strike towers in New York City.' I didn't realize at the time she was predicting the horrors of 9/11; I just thought, 'She's been watching *The Towering Inferno* again.'

Kenny's merchandise may have shattered my childhood innocence, but Kenny the TV comic was going from strength to strength. He was tremendously talented and, as my mother fondly remembers, deeply funny all the time. But harnessing his talent for a half-hour television series still took some doing, and by all accounts it was my father who was mainly responsible. Barry Cryer remembers: 'Ray was pretty much directing the show.'

Kenny's co-star, Cleo Rocos, recalls, 'Ray was the heartbeat of the show. Kenny wouldn't be Kenny without him. He was the pioneer and driving force.' Dad had become a major player in the comedy industry, unofficially writing, directing and producing one of the biggest shows on television, but officially he was just a co-writer. It was time to make a career move.

So my dad took a giant showbusiness leap. He made a film. The film was called *Star Wars*. If only. The film was called *Bloodbath at the House of Death*. He wrote, directed, produced, edited, appeared in and raised the finance for it, quite a step-up from television co-writer. If it came off, we'd be rich. The film starred Kenny Everett at the height of his powers, the legendary Vincent Price ('Darkness falls across the land . . .'), Kenny's TV sidekick Cleo Rocos and Billy Connolly's wife, Pamela Stephenson.

Last week I met Billy Connolly, a hero of mine, at an awards ceremony. I was very nervous about introducing myself. I thought he may remember my father, as he himself appeared on *The Kenny Everett Show* and his missus starred in my dad's movie, but not for a moment did I think he'd recognize me. I loitered near him while he was talking to the comedian Rob Brydon, and then he caught my eye. 'Youu, it's you!' he hollered as only Billy Connolly can.

'Hello, Billy Connolly,' I said, more posh than usual (I always get posher when I'm nervous).

'I was on the train last year,' said The Big Yin, 'and I saaw *Time Out* magazine. The headline was "King of Comedy", big letters. And it was YOU. It was fuckin' youu! King of Comedy? I've never fuckin' heard of you. Who is this guy? I thought. I'm the King of Comedy. I spat out ma sandwich. I'm sittin' there with bits of sandwich on my newspaper and in ma beard.' Billy Connolly knew who I was because he didn't know who I was. I was thrilled nevertheless.

We then had a photo taken, which consisted of, from left to right, Ronnie Corbett, Rob Brydon, myself and Billy Connolly. Referring to our heights, the photographer said, 'Look, you're getting bigger and bigger.'

To which I replied, 'In talent.' That's another thing that happens when I'm nervous. I get a bit cheeky and arrogant.

'Who said that? Who said that?' cried Corbett.

'The King of Comedy strikes again,' sarcastically noted Connolly. We had a brief and nice chat, but I could sense he thought I was posh, cheeky and arrogant. He vaguely remembered my dad, but when I brought up *Bloodbath at the House of Death*, he simply said, 'Pamela's been in a lot of shit movies.' I think that pretty much sums up how my dad's film was received.

For all the hope and hype, he may have bitten off more than he could chew.

The film was a horror spoof. The strap line was 'The film it took a lot of guts to make'. I think that towards the end of filming the budget may have been a bit tight. The final scene of the film is an *E.T.* spoof: a spaceship departing and E.T. running through the woods. The spaceship leaves without him, and E.T. says, 'Oh shit, not again!'

My reasoning for suggesting there may have been financial issues with the production is that the voice-over artist my dad hired to play E.T. was a six-year-old. Me. I had only recently been speaking in sentences that didn't involve the words 'Ma', 'Da' and 'Shums', and here I was doing voice-overs. And swearing. I was a pretty cool six-year-old.

When people met me and asked, 'Are you at school, little man?' I would reply, 'Yeah, but I'm mainly involved in the film industry. I do impressions, mainly extraterrestrial at the moment but I'm looking to diversify.'

Prior to the film's release, everything seemed to be on the up. My parents' Capris were replaced by BMWs, and when the Junkins moved out of London, we bought their flat and also convinced the owner of the remaining flat in the building to sell. We suddenly owned this massive Hampstead house. Well, we actually owned three flats in a massive Hampstead house. We had three kitchens and a million bedrooms, and my sister and I had unimaginable amounts of fun running around it. Kids love to play house – well, until the renovations started, we each had our own apartment. Suddenly I was a voice-over artist with my own place in Hampstead. I was a great catch when I was six. I didn't know at the time that it would take me over twenty-five years to be doing so well again.

My parents, however, were not getting on. I know they argued a great deal, but I only really remember one row in particular. It seemed so trivial. Lucy and I could hear the yelling from our respective flats and even as little people couldn't understand why they would be arguing over such a thing. Grapefruit. My dad was livid over the fact that there was no grapefruit for breakfast. I suppose when two people reach a point when they can't stand each other, they argue over everything. Although remembering the Florida Hilton coffee quarrel, maybe Dad was just very argumentative at breakfast-time. It got pretty heated – I think a La Sorpresa vase may have been smashed at some point. Looking back, the way Mum was shopping in Waitrose, Temple Fortune, it's a wonder there was any food in the house at all, let alone grapefruit.

Parents try to protect their children, so I wasn't fully aware of their problems. As a child, your parents are the two people you love most in the world. To hear them fighting is horribly confusing and upsetting. As I sat on the stairs listening to them arguing, I didn't know that in just two school sports days' time, I would have two dads in the fathers' race (and still no Kenny Everett).

6

I am not superstitious in any way, I don't believe in anything supernatural or paranormal. Fortune-tellers, mediums, psychics are all, in my opinion, nonsense. I've watched those 'talking to the dead' shows, and they just don't make any sense to me. The medium calls out common letters, 'I'm getting a G.'

Then several people in the audience start responding: 'It's Gary', 'It's Gordon', 'It's Grandma.'

If the medium could talk to the dead, why are the dead only giving him the first letter of their name? This is an amazing opportunity for the dead. They must have a lot to talk about, and some pretty major information like: what happens when you die? Is there a God? What's the meaning of life? No, apparently they would rather play some kind of afterlife version of 'Guess Who?' Also, the letters the medium gets are always very common, to give himself the best chance of a response. You'll never see one of these shows when the psychic says, 'I'm getting an "X"', to a silent audience.

Until a French widow stands up and says, 'That must be Xavier!'

When my mother lived alone in Kensington Church Street, very soon after meeting my father at his auditions, she wandered into a psychic bookshop a few doors down from her. She'd walked past it almost every day, but today found herself browsing the occult. There were Tarot card readers in the back, and, with time to kill, she was enticed into a reading. She was young, impressionable and open-minded. Rather than a mystical woman in flowing robes leaning over a small candlelit table, her reader was a relatively normal-looking man. She turned the cards over, and the card reader was immediately shocked by what he saw. My mother was a little concerned by his reaction. 'Is everything OK?' she enquired.

'Can you just wait there a second?' Without waiting for a response, he left her sitting there alone. She started to panic, and by the time he returned had not only convinced herself she was dying, but had doodled a 'Will' on a receipt from her handbag.

The Tarot card reader had brought mystics who worked in the shop to view the cards. All four of them had similarly excitable reactions. 'What is it?' my mother asked.

Her original reader spoke: 'You are pregnant.'

'I'm not,' insisted my mum. In actual fact, she was, but didn't know it yet. Most people find out they're pregnant from a missed period, a home pregnancy test or a big tummy. It's rare to learn this from a Tarot card reader in the back of a psychic bookshop.

'You will have a son,' continued one of the other readers who had been summoned. 'He will be world-famous, everybody will know his name, he will do wonderful things. He is special.'

The rest of her reading contained equally far-fetched information about her future. 'You will have many children. You will live in an old house for five years, and then you and your husband will be separated by the seas and by death. That will be £6.50, please.'

My mother left the bookshop in a trance and went immediately to Boots the chemist just around the corner. It briefly crossed her mind that maybe the Tarot readers have a deal with Boots whereby they predict certain things that send people immediately to the chemist – 'You are pregnant', 'You have a cold sore coming', 'Your hair will go grey' – to boost sales of Clear Blue, Zovirax and Just For Men. My mum purchased the pregnancy test and rushed home. It was positive.

She was overcome with the romance of what had just occurred and clutched her stomach. She felt like the Virgin Mary. 'I am carrying a special son,' she thought to herself. If she gave birth to a baby girl, the whole thing would have been off. But I was born a boy (although slightly camp).

As more and more of the Tarot card reader's predictions came true, my mother became convinced I was some special chosen child. It impacted a bit on my relationship with her when I was a child. Once at dinner I jokingly replaced my glass of water with a glass of Blue Nun, and she crossed herself, fell to the floor and started kissing my feet. At parent–teacher evenings when she was told that I wasn't fulfilling my potential and that I was lazy, she wouldn't really care, remembering Jesus was a carpenter until his thirties. As long as I was achieving in Woodwork, she wasn't bothered about English and Maths. The Tarot card revelations certainly affected me. I was about five or six years old and was learning about the world around me. She had only recently delivered the Tooth Fairy/Easter Bunny/Father Christmas triple blow, when she told me I would grow up to be famous.

It gave me confidence when I was young. I felt that I had a magical secret and that I was special. My mother recently told me that she often thought of the mystical bookshop, which spookily closed down soon after her visit, and wondered as I grew up what path to fame I would take. When I became a successful comedian, I said to her, 'I'm famous now, Mum, just like you said I would be. Are you proud?'

To which she said: 'I was hoping you'd make some kind of medical breakthrough, a cure for a disease or something.'

It's a shame the Tarot card reader couldn't have been a bit more specific: 'You are carrying a child, a son. He will become an observational comedian. I see great importance in the words "Man" and "Drawer".'

Whereas my mother is a believer, I am a sceptic. Every once in a while these psychics are going to get lucky. It's statistics. Maybe the person who visited the bookshop immediately after my mother was also predicted fame and fortune and then got hit by a bus on Kensington High Street moments later. If I'm honest, I'd rather it wasn't true anyway – I'm not a fan of destiny. What's the point of living your life if it's all mapped out ahead of you? And if these Tarot card readers were so accurate, why couldn't they foresee their bookshop closing down? Anyway, if the Tarot reader's prophecies were to come true, there was to be strife before my glittering future. If we were to 'live in an old house for five years', our time was nearly up, and the 'separated by seas and death' prediction was a bit of a worry.

It certainly didn't seem like we were about to move from Hampstead. We were in the process of developing our three flats into one big house. I remember living with builders for some time. Our lives were dominated by workmen shouting, sledgehammers smashing, skips loading, wheelbarrows wheeling and dust billowing. My sister, whose own oracle-like qualities seemed to be confined to the destruction of buildings, babbled constantly about walls and ceilings tumbling. The builders were fun and friendly, probably due to my mum. My mum was the type of lady at whom builders whistle. Builders' whistles often fall on deaf ears, but now when they whistled, my mum would bring them tea. I remember one of them, Steve, inviting me to punch him in the stomach. This was wildly exciting for me. Steve was like a real live He-Man. 'What? As hard as I can?' I questioned, overestimating my own seven-year-old strength.

'Sure,' Steve confidently replied. So I swung with all my might and connected flush with Steve's rock-like stomach. He didn't even flinch. I couldn't believe it. I hit him again, this time with a run-up, but he barely noticed. It was like living with the Incredible Hulk. My friends would come to my house just to punch him in the stomach.

One of my friends, Barnaby, accidentally punched the wrong builder in the stomach – 'Oi! Fuck off, you little shit.' Barnaby burst into tears and didn't come round again.

The house itself soon started to take shape and began to be decorated. Because it was the mid-eighties, my mother settled upon a theme for her lovely new home. Hideous. An expression I heard a lot when growing up and, thankfully never again, was 'rag-rolling'. 'Rag-rolling' is when you take a painted wall and ruin it. I can only imagine it was invented by mistake. Someone in the eighties must have leant on a wall without realizing it was newly painted and in the process not only invented 'rag-rolling', but also the equally tasteless paint-splattered shirt which was all the rage at the time. What was wrong with people in the 1980s? I think the singer Sade was the only person who looked good.

My mother was looking less like Bananarama and more like Krystle Carrington every day. Her shoulder pads were so large she was once late picking me up from school because one of them wedged in the door of her new BMW 3-Series. The builders had to widen the doorways so she could get around her own home. She used every fad going to create what in the eighties was a dream home, but in hindsight was the stuff of nightmares. Looking back, I'd rather have lived in my father's fictional 'House of Death'. Loud bright colours were the order of the day. The out-of-bounds dark living room now had sky-blue rag-rolled walls and custard yellow carpets. Even though I was now allowed in, I banned myself from entering. The kitchen walls were Barbara Cartland pink with white stripes. Upstairs was worse. My mum employed more painting techniques of the era. There was a lot of 'stencilling' in the bedrooms and 'marbling' in the bathrooms. Marbling was painting made to look like marble. The results were criminal. A couple of the bedrooms were stencilled with swirls that were so disorientating it was difficult to keep your balance.

The fittings and fixtures were even more offensive. We had white cowboy doors between the pink kitchen and peach dining room. It was like a scene from the alternative ending of *Brokeback Mountain*, the version where they live happily ever after. The pièce de résistance of our new Hampstead house of horrors was undoubtedly the master bathroom. The bath had golden taps beside a spout in the shape of a swan's neck and head. The water would shoot out of the swan's mouth, like it was vomiting. The black loo was so over-stylized that it was actually unusable. The loo seat was angled in such a way that it pushed one's bottom cheeks together, thus blocking nature's course. It was difficult enough to poo with a vomiting gold swan staring at you, but the design fault made it physically impossible. It became a 'show loo', just for decoration. The whole house was a bit like that.

I don't remember my father being around while the work was being done. He must have been making or editing his film. I know that he was also travelling to America a lot as he was putting together the sketch show *Assaulted Nuts*, which was co-produced by the US cable network HBO.

What I do remember is sitting in our newly con-verted loft playing with excess rolls of carpet and coming across my mother's Filofax (an eighties must-have) and seeing a note to her from Steve, the builder with an iron chest. 'I love you,' it read. Why would Steve the builder love my mum? I was shocked. At this moment, my mother walked in. 'Have you seen my Filofax, darling?' She saw me sitting on the fluffy new carpet, the blood drained from my young face. 'Are you all right, Michael?'

'No,' I said, barely audible. 'The room is spinning.'

'I know, Michael, that's the stencilling. That's the effect I'm going for. You'll get used to it, it's very trendy.'

I showed her the Filofax. 'What's that mean?' I asked fearfully. Unfortunately, it had flicked to another page, 21 June.

'The summer solstice,' she explained. 'That's the first day of summer, I think.'

'No,' I said, riffling through the Filofax to find the incriminating page. 'That. What does that mean?'

I thought confronting my mother with evidence of her adultery would be dramatic, but it was nothing of the sort. 'I love Steve, we love each other. I thought you knew that.'

I genuinely couldn't believe how blasé she was being. 'No, I didn't.'

'We've been together for a while. Why do you think he's always here?'

'To decorate,' I said truthfully.

My mum chose to downplay the gravity of the situation. Either that or she was so in love with the builder that she was blissfully unaware that she was married with two kids. I thought for a moment that maybe these avant-garde painting techniques were responsible for my mother's seduction. She did seem to be in a trance-like state. Maybe she was just Steve's latest victim, and he was some kind of decorating Derren Brown using a combination of rag-rolling, stencilling and marbling in a series of gaudy colours to hypnotize housewives.

My memories of our final days in Hampstead are not only hazy, but also confused by the fact that a lot was kept from Lucy and me to 'protect' us. This was a messy divorce with kids involved, and I was one of the kids. My dad came back from America to a strange and hostile environment. I can't imagine what it must have been like for my father. A man's first instinct when he learns his wife is cheating on him is to attack the other man. 'Who is it? Where is he?' Unfortunately in this instance, it was Steve, the iron-chested builder. My dad could have punched Steve repeatedly in the stomach, and Steve wouldn't even have noticed – he would have just carried on rag-rolling while listening to his Sony Walkman. Your partner cheating on you is bad enough. If she cheats on you with a bigger man, it's the worst-case scenario. What are you supposed to do when you catch them together? 'Hey, that's my wife. Get off her or I'll hit you, and then you'll hit me and I'll be hospitalized.'

What if your partner cheats on you with a hero of yours? At the time of writing John Terry has just lost his England captaincy for alleged adultery. But what if he was sleeping with the wife of a Chelsea season ticket holder who proudly wears a John Terry replica shirt, and it's days before the European Cup Final? What would be the husband's reaction then? Initially he would be shocked and angered by the infidelity of his wife before noticing his idol in his bed. 'How could you do it this to me, you fu— There's only one John Terry, one

John Teeeeery, there's only one John Terry. Look who it is, love, it's JT!'

'I know, I'm having sex with him.'

'You all right, JT? Can I get you some water or something? He's got the final on Wednesday night, so you should go on top, love. He's got to save his energy. Careful, darling, mind his metatarsal, that's six weeks out, that is.'

The marriage was over. They weren't happy. My dad was working hard, my mum was playing hard, and when they were together they were arguing hard. They were from different generations and the gap was never going to close. A friend of my mum said to her at the time of the separation, 'Children grow up and leave home, and that's all you're doing.'

My grandmother was thrilled to learn that the marriage was over and swigged from a glass of fine champagne. 'Daarling, you are doing the right thing, he vas no gud for you. Start egen, I vill help you vith money.' Then my mum told her about Steve. She choked, vintage champagne spluttered from her mouth and through her nose 'Vot? The builder? I'm feeling faint, Jim, Jim, get my pills . . .'

I haven't really gone into much detail about Grandma's rich husband Jim. For all his business prowess and swollen bank account, he was very much a secondary figure in my grandmother's home. He acted and looked like a butler, very English, very proper, very upright.

He occasionally smirked or scowled, hinting towards true feelings that he never voiced. He fetched my grandma's pills. 'You're telling me you are in luv with the rag-rohleeer?' she continued. 'Vell, you vont get a bean out of me. He is after the money, and he's not getting any.' My grandmother believed everybody was after her money.

In hindsight, I think my parents' marriage breakdown was inevitable. I've met them both, and they genuinely had nothing in common. I'm surprised it lasted as long as it did. Although my mum was spending a lot of time with Kenny and his friends, it was only a matter of time before she met a heterosexual man. People who are single are often encouraged to 'get out there, don't just wait for Mr Right to come knocking on your door'. Well, in my mother's case, Mr Right smashed the door down, installed a new one, then painted and rag-rolled it. They were in love and determined to start a life together, a life with Lucy and me. My home was broken. The Hampstead house was put on the market.

Let's just put the divorce to one side for a moment. Park the divorce. I want to talk about house prices. It was 1983 and we owned a substantial house in Hampstead. I also want you to put the décor of the house to one side. Park the décor. Park it next to the divorce.

Because of a wonderful website, with which I became obsessed when I was house hunting called houseprices.co.uk, you can now find out the price of homes sold anywhere in the UK. We sold our Hampstead house in 1983 for £330,000, a substantial amount of money at the time, even today. At the peak of the market in 2007, the same house was sold for £4.2 million. Here's a question: why the fuck didn't the Tarot card reader mention that? The house increased in value by £160,000 a year. Would this knowledge have saved my parents' marriage? (I've just un-parked the divorce.) I don't think so. But maybe it would have prevented them from selling their goldmine with hideous interior. (I've just un-parked the décor.) For that kind of money, Steve could have built a dividing wall and they could have split the house. Lucy and I would still live with both our parents, and in twenty-five years we would all walk away millionaires.

It wasn't to be. The house was sold, bizarrely, to the Osbournes. Any relation? Yes, it was them, the actual Osbournes. Sharon and Ozzy and little baby Jack. Kelly Osbourne had just been born at the time. This is from Sharon's autobiography: 'Ozzy arrived for the birth and I took him to see somewhere I found in Hampstead. It was Victorian, semi-detached with a garden, not enormous but somewhere to put the pram . . . It needed a lot doing to it, but the price was good and it had great potential.'

This is an historic moment: the overlapping of two celebrity autobiographies. It's interesting, the different perspectives. For Sharon, the house was 'not enormous';

for me, it was 'enormous'. Sharon felt it 'needed a lot doing to it'; for me, it was 'hideous'. It also said in her book that it was the first place that felt like a family home. The house certainly had the potential to be one; unfortunately, we were the wrong family. I doubt that when my father bought all the different flats and sat down with his architect, he said, 'I want to create the perfect family home, for the Prince of Darkness.'

I had obviously never heard of Ozzy Osbourne. It may not come as a shock to you to learn that I never went through a 'heavy metal' phase. For all I knew, Black Sabbath was just another date in my mum's Filofax. Before the MTV television series that endeared Ozzy and his family to the world, he was primarily known for eating the head of a bat. When my mother told me to tidy my room 'because a man who bites the heads off bats is coming round to look at it', I thought it was a threat. I've never cleaned my room so well in my life. Inspired by my mother's Capri cleaning, I usually just threw rubbish out of the window, but this time I had the place immaculate. 'All right, I'll do it! Please don't let the man bite my head off.'

The proceeds of the house sale were divided equally between my parents so each could start a new life. My father rented a house belonging to friends in Hertford-shire, and my mum, Steve, Lucy and I bought a house in Golders Green. So that was it, a new chapter in my life was beginning. Annoyingly, this is my autobiography and I haven't actually reached the end of the chapter – bad planning on my part. I feel I need to introduce Steve to you properly, as he now looks all set to become my stepfather. No, maybe I should end the chapter here.

I think I will.

7

A new chapter in my life had begun. I didn't know it at the time, but it was Chapter 7. There was a new man in my mother's life, and because I was only seven years old and Lucy five, there was a new man in ours as well. We were the baggage that my mother came with.

Steve was pretty much the same age as my mum and looked almost identical to Patrick Swayze. Much to his embarrassment, his mother entered him in a Patrick Swayze look-alike contest by sending in a photo. He came second. I genuinely don't know how he didn't win; either it was rigged or the real Patrick Swayze entered. Steve was often mistaken for the Hollywood star in the most unlikely locations. 'Oh my God, are you Patrick Swayze?'

'No, do you really think Patrick Swayze would be buying paint in Wickes on the North Circular? Oh, look over there! It's Tom Selleck looking at drills.'

Steve was young, more *Point Break* than *Donnie Darko*. He was an aspiring painter in the artistic sense but was painting in the painter/decorator sense to make ends meet. He grew up in Brixton with its predominantly West Indian community. He spoke in Jive as a party trick. His father was an electrician and his mother a dental nurse. On his first day of school he wore shorts, not knowing that the 'all boys should wear shorts' rule was ignored by every other boy at the school. This trouser-length faux pas led to him being ridiculed and locked all day in the cupboard that housed the fuse boxes and electrical meters. When Steve finally made it home, his father asked, 'How was your first day at school?'

'Much like your day at work, Dad, except I didn't have a torch,' he replied. The following day, now wearing trousers, he approached the largest of the bullies who had locked him up and punched him in the mouth, knocking several teeth out.

The father of his now front-toothless victim squared up to Steve's father at the end of school. 'Hey, your kid has knocked my kid's teeth out.'

'What do you want me to do about it? I'm an electrician,' was Steve's father's now legendary response. 'You want my wife for that. She'll book you in for an appointment with the dentist.'

For all the punching in the stomach and 'history of violence' on his first day at school, Steve was and is the gentlest man I have ever met. He likes stamp-collecting and bird-watching and is extraordinarily passive and sweet-natured. Lucy and I liked him immediately. You might have expected the opposite reaction. Here was a man breaking up my family. But I didn't see it that way. My parents were so unsuited to each other. It was now

My mum, Kati Katz, a teenage
pregnancy waiting to happen.

An early publicity shot of new Canadian
comedian Ray Cameron, my dad.

'Hellooo Daaarlings!' My glamour Gran.

Me, during my brief stint as an East End Crime Lord.

My mother wondering whether she'd accidentally
picked up a Super Mario Brother from the hospital.

My dad and me eating breakfast in bed – the scene of his morning-breath cuddles.

On the top bunk with my sister Lucy, where she correctly predicted the ceiling would fall down.

Lucy and me in the bath in Hampstead. Check out the wallpaper and the tassles on the side of the bath, not to mention the razors within easy reach of children.

In my garden in Hampstead, trying to get away from Lucy and our neighbour Annabelle in a scene not dissimilar to *The Shining*.

When my parents weren't loving, teaching and raising me, they liked to dress me up as chart toppers from the 70s.

Kenny Everett, in Sid Snot guise, with Barry Cryer and my dad in their heyday, caught in a rare moment not laughing at each other's jokes.

Dad and the legendary actor Vincent Price on the set of *Bloodbath at the House of Death*. Known for his quirky unconventional directing style, my father insisted that his crew should be holding a polystyrene cup at all times.

'Wine, women . . .' I think it was more like 'Champagne, men . . .' Kenny and my mum, going by the name Marianne, just back from Waitrose.

WINE, women – and now song. Kenny Everett's got the lot! He and friend Marianne are pictured celebrating his new job with London's Capital Radio after the BBC had fired him for the second time.   © The Sun and 01.06.1984 / nisyndication.com

Here I am in my trademark suit with my mum and Kenny on her birthday.

My family. All together.

warfare. The last thing I wanted was for them to be together. How can two people who hate each other make a happy home?

Our Golders Green house was built in the 1930s. It required some work, but Steve was determined to do it all himself, not just to save money but also because his new girlfriend had a history of sleeping with contracted builders. It was detached with four bedrooms, a small kitchen, small living room, dining room and one bathroom. It was perfect for a young Jewish family. The main drawback was that none of us were Jewish. My mother's father was Jewish (remember Laszlo, the Hungarian scientist whose sister's son was Uncle Peter, the guy who gassed himself in the face?), but one Jewish relative is not enough to make you particularly welcome in the neighbourhood.

Although the house was a good size for the money, He-Man builder Steve could easily do any work necessary, and though it was only about two miles from our old Hampstead house, it was like moving abroad. I felt a bit like Harrison Ford in *Witness*. Golders Green is properly Orthodox Jewish. Everyone has skullcaps, long hair with side-curls, all black clothing and Volvos. Volvos are very popular with Jewish people; they refuse to buy German cars (with good reason) so BMWs, Mercedes, Audis, Volkswagens and Porsches are all out of the question. There are of course many other good-quality cars that aren't German, but everybody in Golders

Green seems to go for the Swedish Volvo. The Volvo, of course, is famed for being the safest and strongest vehicle on the road, so if they saw a Nazi, they could run him over with minimal risk to themselves.

I don't think we did ourselves many favours when we first arrived in my mother's new BMW 3-Series with Kraftwerk playing on the stereo. Adjacent to our new home was some outside space, a park that my mother christened 'Dog Shit Park'. She told the neighbours she'd christened it 'Dog Shit Park', but they just slammed the door: 'We don't believe in Christ.' The council wasn't as stringent with dog fouling in those days. In the mid-eighties most of the dogs didn't even have collars, as all the punks were wearing them.

Golders Green's high street was an excellent shopping parade, if you're kosher. There are shops and bakeries that not only seem to have been there since the beginning of time, but have the same people in them. Grodzinski's was a coffee shop that had the same collection of old Jewish ladies, in the same seats, sipping the same coffee, every time I walked past. The high street seems to be in some kind of a time warp. Chains of shops would go out of business elsewhere but remain open in Golders Green. I think today there are still a C&A, Wimpy, Cecil Gee, Woolworths and Our Price.

The best thing about Golders Green, and the reason I still go back, is the I. Warman-Freed chemist. Most chemists keep regular business hours. Boots, for example, is usually open from 8.30 a.m. to 6 p.m. So you have to fall ill, or require any form of medication or remedy, between these hours. If you have a cold sore and want to adhere to the advert that tells you to buy Zovirax 'at the first sign of tingling', you can't outside certain times. In fact between 6 p.m. and 8.30 a.m., every ailment known to man must be treated with Nurofen from the petrol station or a visit to Casualty. It's a wonder this situation is tolerated. Well, there is one group of people who would never tolerate such a state of affairs. Jews. Which is why smack-bang in the middle of Golders Green Road is I. Warman-Freed, the all-night chemist. I don't know who I. Warman-Freed was, but he certainly understood the neuroses of Jewish people. You know when the *Harry Potter* books are released and people of all ages queue around the block? Well, the I. Warman-Freed pharmacy counter is like that twenty-four hours a day.

During the week, I lived in Golders Green in what felt like an FBI witness relocation 'safe house'. On the weekends Lucy and I would stay with our dad in his temporary accommodation. Strangely, it's from this point on that my memories of my father are much stronger. He was obviously very busy with work prior to the divorce, but now in his 'weekend dad' capacity, he made the most of our time together. Being apart from his kids was heartbreaking for him and he desperately wanted to make us feel we had a new home with him as well as in Israel – sorry, Golders Green. Seemingly within minutes of his separation from my mother, there was a new lady in his life.

While my mother was being romanced in plaster of Paris by Steve in scenes not dissimilar to the film *Ghost*, my father had met a twenty-seven-year-old Floridian sweetheart during his frequent visits to America. I'm not aware of the details; all I remember is that Lucy and I went to visit him in his rented cottage, and there she was, Holly Hughes.

The best way accurately to describe Holly is that she was 'American'. She had rosy cheeks and wore leggings with baggy T-shirts. She was bubbly and confident and in love with my dad. It was extraordinary, after some home renovations and a business trip, I suddenly had two mums and two dads. Holly had been working in the music business and from what I remember had been very successful.

She brought American culture into my life for the first time. I say 'culture'; I mean 'food'. Holly introduced us children to a standard of eating that would have had Jamie Oliver pressing charges. 'Jiffy Pop' was a highlight; this was basically a saucepan-shaped package that you heated on the hob until it created a big aluminium (a word she couldn't pronounce) balloon filled with popcorn. 'Sloppy Joes' were a lowlight; these were hamburger buns covered in a sort of super-sweet Bolognese sauce. I don't know who 'Sloppy Joe' was, but he was almost certainly clinically obese, and so would Lucy and I have been if our dad had won custody. In general, Lucy and I loved Holly's weekend cooking, and her hot chocolate is the best I've ever tasted.

This split lifestyle that Lucy and I were leading had some major perks. My dad was definitely trying to make up for his enforced absence by spoiling us. He bought us top-of-the-range BMXs to explore the Hertfordshire countryside. My metallic blue Raleigh Burner was the love of my life thus far. Lucy and I were kitted out with all the latest cycling accessories: helmets, gloves, knee and elbow pads, flashing lights and sirens. We looked like something from outer space. I actually think some of the local farmers reported alien sightings.

My dad was certainly flush with cash at this point, and apart from our lavish divorce-inspired gifts he purchased himself a gorgeous silver BMW 635 CSI. I don't know what the 'CSI' stood for, but it was top of the range and had something to do with making it go faster – either that or the previous owner was murdered in it. The major excitement about his new car was that it had a phone in it. Nowadays, everyone has a phone on them all the time. But in 1984 it was tremendously state of the art. People saw car phones as the future of technology (the Carphone Warehouse did, but they now sell as many car phones as Blockbuster Video sells videos).

My dad's car phone was the envy of all my friends,

and all his friends for that matter. It was long and sleek and sat proudly next to the handbrake. Unfortunately, it was also about the same size as the handbrake, which led to dangerous mishaps. When the phone rang, he would pick up the handbrake by mistake, sending the car into a spin. Or he would stop on a hill, reach for the handbrake, but pick up the phone by mistake and roll into the car behind. The phone itself barely had a signal, and when he got one the conversation would only last long enough for him to say he was in the car. 'Hi, I'm in the car, I'm on the car pho– Hello?' It was basically a device for informing people he was driving.

My sister and I loved his BMW 6-Series. On a Friday afternoon, Daddy would pick us up from school in his magnificent sports saloon. We would hurtle up the M1 motorway at law-breaking speeds. Lucy and I would pick cars ahead of us to overtake while I would be shouting out our speed, '116, 117 . . . 120 miles an hour!' It's only looking back that I realize just how dangerous this was, not to mention highly illegal. I know it sounds strange, but our dad was using the car to bond with us. He was desperate. He had lost his kids for five days of the week, and he had to make up ground, at 120 miles per hour. He had to cram a lot into his two days and wanted to make us happy. So if that involved expensive presents and treating the motorway like a Grand Prix track, so be it.

The BMW 6-Series happened to be my mum's dream

car. She had a 3-Series, but every time we drove past a 6-Series, she would state her intent: 'I love that car, I want one.' She likes cars, my mum. In general, she's a pretty good driver, despite the lack of seat belt and occasional magazine-reading. Where her driving falls down, however, is at the set of traffic lights on the Finchley Road at the junction with West End Lane. Her misunderstanding of the filter light system resulted in three collisions in the very same place.

The insurance company kept saying to her, 'You've already told us about this accident.'

To which she would shamefully reply, 'I'm sorry, I've done it again.' Unfortunately, this junction was on the school run. Lucy and I would have to brace for impact twice a day.

Even though things were tight financially and Steve was searching for a more substantial job, when my mother received some money from her late father's estate, she decided to blow it on a BMW 6-Series. The problem was that she only had £7,000 to spend. My dad's 6-Series had cost closer to £25,000. Thanks to *Autotrader* or *Loot* or something of that ilk, we found one for £6,995. It was a light blue 633i with plenty of miles on the clock and fewer extras than my BMX Raleigh Burner, but it was a 6-Series (although it may have been two 3-Series welded together). It was perfect. We spent the £5 change on petrol and went on one of those 'new car drives' where you aren't actually going anywhere, just cruising around. Unfortunately, because we lived in London, we got stuck in roadworks for an hour and a half and reached a top speed of 7 mph. Typical.

The sensible decision was taken not to tell my grandmother about the 6-Series. Her reaction would not have been: 'Good vor you, luvely car, fuel injection, wery classy, you deserve, mast get burglar gassing device, very populer in Hungaaary.' It would more likely have been: 'You blow money on ztupid car, you vasters, I will cut you out of my vill.' She tended to use her money as a weapon, and threatened to cut us out of her 'vill' about every thirty to forty minutes. 'Michael, come end give yur grenny a hug, or I vill cut you out of my vill.' 'These kerritz are burned, Kati, I vill cut you out of my vill.'

We were the poor relations, and Grandma revelled in it. When she visited, she would bring us food from her fridge that had passed its use-by date as a gift. Whenever she found loose change on our floor or behind the sofa, she would accuse my mother of wasting money and would preach her mantra: 'Look avter ze pennies and ze pounds vill take care of themselves', forgetting that marrying a millionaire also helps. So the decision was taken to keep the new car a secret. When we visited her, we would drive our old 3-Series and when she visited us we would hide our new 6-Series up the road. It simply wasn't worth the trouble. Grandma would much rather her daughter was eating out-of-date dinner surrounded by jars of 1ps and 2ps, than cruising around in a new set of wheels.

The first time my mum dropped Lucy and me off at our dad's rented cottage in her light blue 633i BMW, parking it alongside his silver 635 CSI, all hell broke loose. He accused her of purposefully undermining him by buying the same car as him, the car Lucy and I loved so much. It was horrific. The 'grapefruit' row was nothing compared to the 'BMW 6-Series' row. Steve and Holly were both present and embarrassed. They peeled off to one side and chatted awkwardly. 'I gather you brought a lot of Jiffy Pop over from the States, the kids really love it,' Steve said, searching for conversation.

'Are you Patrick Swayze?' replied Holly.

Meanwhile, my parents were screaming at each other in the drive between their respective shiny new BMWs, like an episode of *Top Gear* gone wrong. He was accusing her of buying the car to spite him, and she was adamantly denying it. At the end of the argument, my mum and Steve were ordered off my dad's rented accommodation. 'Come on, Steve, we're leaving,' cried my mother.

To add insult to injury, Steve then got into my dad's BMW by mistake. 'I can't fucking believe this,' commented my dad to Holly.

'Is that Patrick Swayze?' she replied.

Steve and my mum then leapt into the correct car and sped off at an impressive 0–60 in 6.8 seconds. The result of this ugly scene was that my mum was banned from my dad's house. In future, Lucy and I were to be dropped off at a neutral location, the Swan Pub near Hemel Hempstead, to be bundled from one BMW 6-Series to another.

Jewish architect David Rosenberg was another proud new car owner in Golders Green. He had infuriated his neighbours by buying a Mercedes 500SL, a German car. He was a chancer who began selling ice creams in the City before convincing a Japanese customer to let him redesign his offices. He made money wherever the opportunity presented itself. He once shut his own fingers in the door of Barclays Bank and sued them for a small fortune.

He was cunning and crafty, the kind of guy who does well on *The Apprentice* with Lord Alan Sugar, doesn't win, and then gets booed on *The Apprentice – You're Fired* with Adrian Chiles. He was also a terrible driver and had so many accidents he was considering shutting his fingers in another bank door to pay the astronomical insurance premium on his new sporty motor. Steve, my mum, Lucy and I met David in a head-on collision on Redington Road, in Hampstead. Our short and disruptive romance with our seven-grand sports saloon ended just weeks after it had begun.

Lucy and I were in the back, Mum was in the passenger seat, and Steve was driving. Redington Road is a residential road, home to the rich and famous. We had friends living there, the married actors John Alderton and Pauline Collins. John and Pauline's youngest son, Richard, was at school with Lucy and me, and they had hit it off with our mum at the school gates. By sheer co-incidence, David Rosenberg's Mercedes and our BMW crashed directly outside the home of the *Forever Green* stars. They both heard the impact and rushed outside. The scene they found was not pleasant. Both cars were written-off, or 'totalled', as Holly would have said. I had managed to cling on to the seat in front of me, Lucy injured her leg and my mother's head smashed through the windscreen.

Because David Rosenberg had been involved in so many car accidents, his only concern was liability. He jumped out of his broken car, camera in hand, photo-graphing the crash site. He was collecting evidence. Hilariously, these photos were self-incriminating because his car was clearly on the wrong side of the road. So while the stars of *Please, Sir* and *Shirley Valentine* were recovering us from the wreckage, David Rosenberg was busy prov-ing beyond all reasonable doubt that the accident was his fault.

Distraught and slightly concussed, my mother tele-phoned my grandmother and told her about the accident. Thank God, everyone had escaped with only minor injuries. The car, however, was unsalvageable. She totally forgot that Grandma was unaware we owned the car involved. It still hadn't dawned on her when Grandma and Jim came round the following day with a bag full of goodies past their use-by date, to console us. They were twenty minutes late so I peeked out of the window to find them in our driveway, circling the 3-Series inspecting the non-existent damage. I ran downstairs. 'Grandma and Grandpa are outside.'

'Why don't you let them in?' Steve said.

'They're inspecting the 3-Series. Why did you leave it in the drive?'

'Shiiiiit,' my mum screamed. At that moment the doorbell went. 'What am I going to say?' They had put themselves in the awkward position of having to explain how their unsalvageable car had been miraculously restored to its former state in less than twenty-four hours. They briefly considered climbing over the garden fence and making a run for it, but Lucy's bruised leg wasn't up to it. The doorbell sounded again. My mother finally opened the door.

'Helloo, daaarling, ze car it is fine. Vot is going on?' My mother began lying through her teeth. She explained how the crash wasn't as bad as she first thought.

Steve chipped in with the classic line, 'The damage was mainly internal.'

Grandma and Jim didn't believe a word of it and pretty soon the truth came out. 'You vucking liars, I'm cutting you out of my vill,' she yelled as she sped off.

Grandma wasn't speaking to us, the car only had third-party insurance so was lost, and Steve was struggling to find a job to support his new family. The BMW

633i had caused nothing but trouble. But then, out of the light blue, the 6-Series saga had a happy ending. David Rosenberg had perused his photos of the crash and realized he was the guilty party and his insurers would punish him for this. He regretted taking the photos, but treasured the one of him and John Alderton, one of his favourite actors. David popped over to our house to discuss the situation.

He was charming and very keen to strike a deal with my mum and Steve. Making polite conversation, they found themselves discussing David's new business venture. He had recently founded a new architectural company and purchased a snazzy new computer design system and was looking for somebody to operate it. 'What a coincidence,' lied the job-hunting Steve, 'I can do that.' A visit to WHSmith and a few days' and nights' cramming later, Steve landed himself a job at David's company. He worked there for the next ten years.

8

Some time during my domestic turmoil, I started 'big boy' school. I went to a lovely school called Arnold House in St John's Wood, London. I wore a bright red blazer with dark trim. It looked like a ladybird costume. Unlike Steve's first day, when he was beaten and locked in a cupboard for wearing shorts, everybody in the Arnold House Junior School obeyed the rules and wore tiny little shorts, like the ones worn by footballers in the seventies. At break-time there were more goose pimples in the playground than on a battery farm in the Arctic. Matters were made even worse for me as my mum put my shorts in the wrong wash, not only shrinking them but also giving them a slightly golden sheen after they shared the machine with one of her *Dynasty*-inspired trouser suits. I was going to school in hot pants looking a bit like Kylie Minogue in the 'Spinning Around' video.

Arnold House is a private all-boys school and cost my father a fortune. It was oddly formal. I remember referring to all my friends by their second names. My best friend, Sam Geddes, was known as Geddes, and I was McIntyre. The school register in the morning sounded like a list of advertising agencies. Teachers had no names at all and were called 'sir' or 'miss'. When the teacher walked into the classroom, all the boys would stand up until 'sir' told them to 'Be seated.' What's that all about? It's the wrong way around. I'm paying a fortune for this school; shouldn't the teacher call me 'sir' and stand up when I walk in?

The school was also a bit religious. Every morning we gathered in the gym for assembly and recited the Lord's Prayer. The headmaster, Mr Clegg, would lead and the teachers and whole school would mumble along: 'Our Father, who art in heaven, hallowed be thy name . . . Give us this day our daily bread . . . And forgive us our trespasses, as we forgive them that trespass against us . . . For thine is the kingdom, the power, and the glory, for ever and ever . . .'

At the end, we'd all very loudly say, 'Amen.' Every day I said this, for six years. I didn't have a clue what it meant and nobody explained it. I remember thinking, 'What daily bread? I had cereal this morning', 'Does this mean I'm allowed to trespass?', 'Why should I forgive people who trespass against me?' There was a grassed area in front of the junior school that had a 'No Trespassing' sign. I used to walk across it safe in the knowledge that God would forgive me.

Academically I was unpredictable. One year I was literally bottom of the class in every subject. I got 4 per cent in French, 7 per cent in History and got lost on the way to the Geography exam. My Maths was so bad that

I didn't actually know what per cent meant. My poor grades may have been due to my problems at home, or simply because I already knew I was going to be wildly successful thanks to the Tarot cards. My mum didn't seem to mind at all.

My end-of-year report was a collection of slips of paper written by the teacher of each subject. It was so awful that I threw most of it in the bin and only gave her PE (Physical Education) and RE (Religious Education). She didn't notice and was thrilled that I had 'a keen interest in Sport' and was 'Very attentive during Bible readings'. It didn't seem to concern her that I was only learning two subjects or that I was all set to be the next David Icke.

My dad, on the other hand, did notice. 'Where's the rest of your report?' He was livid and lectured me for hours on the importance of school, not to mention the astronomical school fees he was paying to keep me there. Something he said to me registered and I became determined to succeed at school. I became a 'swot' overnight. I found out what per cent meant and then gave it one hundred.

I remember the teachers thinking I was stupid, in particular Mrs Orton, the French teacher. She had good reason after my 4 per cent in the exam. Mrs Orton was one of those teachers who was never totally in control of the class. It didn't help that her English was limited and when she wanted us to 'be quiet', she would shout 'Shoot' and then smack the blackboard with the blackboard rubber. I presume she was trying to say 'Shut up', but for some reason it came out of her mouth as 'Shoot!' Every time she said 'Shoot!', the class would giggle, which would only make her repeat 'Shoot!', and again smash the blackboard. For most of the forty-five-minute lesson, she would be shouting, 'Shoot!' and banging the blackboard with its rubber.

Before and after lessons, my friends and I would impersonate Mrs Orton to each other with much hysteria. It was during one of these muckabouts that one of us noticed there was a gap behind the blackboard. The blackboard was positioned against the corner leaving a little space behind it. After a little encouragement, we convinced the smallest kid in the class, Watson, to try and squeeze in. We must have lost track of time because just as he jammed himself between the wall and the blackboard, Mrs Orton entered to begin her French lesson.

Watson ducked down and the rest of us scrambled to our seats. Mrs Orton addressed the class, oblivious to the hiding Watson. We tried to contain ourselves but the situation was too much to bear. Pockets of sniggering broke out. Then Mrs Orton, true to form, smacked her rubber on the blackboard and shouted 'Shoot!' This was probably the first time in my life I properly got the giggles. The whole class fell into total hysterics as she continued to shout 'Shoot!' louder and louder and hit the board harder and harder with Watson wedged behind it. As far as I remember he was in there for the whole lesson.

Even though Mrs Orton never knew why we were laughing, she was always looking at me and singling me out as the culprit of whatever shenanigans were occurring. She saw me as a waster, a loser and an idiot. My 4 per cent just proved her suspicions. But now I was on a mission. I concentrated, I learned. I studied in the school library at break-time, I read my textbooks in the car on the school run, I got my mum and my sister to test me constantly, I played Survivor's 'Eye of the Tiger' as I did my homework.

When the exams came I had never been more prepared for anything in my short life. Still to this day, I remember most of my results. Maths 78 per cent, Geography 87 per cent, History 82 per cent, Science 83 per cent, French 92 per cent. I came top of the class in every subject. My mum was thrilled (but she was thrilled when I only studied PE and RE), my dad was proud, but the person I was most looking forward to seeing was Mrs Orton. From 4 per cent to 92 per cent, quite an improvement. I sat waiting in the classroom for the French lesson to begin, enjoying my newfound status. I was top of the class. I was a champion.

The teacher walked in, but it wasn't Mrs Orton. We were told that she had left the school and this new guy, Mr Sissons, was taking over. It transpired that Mr Sissons marked the exams. Mrs Orton was gone, and she was unaware of my dramatic turn-around. I was truly gutted. Where had she gone? Nobody knew. There was a rumour somebody had finally shot her. About ten years later, I was playing tennis in a park when I heard an unmistakable sound from the next court: 'Shoot!' I looked over and there she was, planting a forehand volley into the net.

I ran over to her, forgetting I was now nineteen years old and a decade had passed. 'Mrs Orton,' I screeched, 'I got 92 per cent.' Naturally, she had no recollection of me whatsoever. I apologized and we continued our respective games.

Academically, that was my one good year. I never again worked so hard or scaled those heights. I suppose I just wanted to prove to myself and to my dad I could reach the top, and having done that I slipped back down to the middle. I never again excelled in any subject. I was a bit like Blackburn Rovers when they won the league in 1992. One subject I certainly never excelled in was Music. I am simply not musical in any way. I can barely press 'play' on the stereo. My dad, of course, had a musical background and was very keen for me to take up an instrument. More specifically, he wanted me to learn the piano. He owned a piano for me to practise on so he was especially keen for this to be my instrument of choice.

My best friend at the time was Gary Johnson. Gary was tremendously cool. He was a fair-haired American, liked basketball and had his own 'ghetto blaster'. When my mum asked him what he wanted to be when he grew up, he said, 'Black.' Gary said guitars were cool, so my mind was made up. The guitar was the only instrument for me. I argued with my dad for hours. The 'guitar' row was our biggest to date, and it was only when I threatened divorce that he eventually backed down. He begrudgingly bought me a guitar and booked me in for lessons at my school. Gary said my guitar wasn't cool – he'd meant electric guitars. So I didn't attend a single lesson. The guitar sat in my Golders Green bedroom in its case, untouched. My dad didn't live with us so he would never know. I was now only seeing him every other weekend. He and Holly were as in love as Steve and my mother, and bought a big country house. She had been living in LA and he in London, but they now decided to pursue an English country life together.

Holly dreamed of an idyllic rural life and my dad set about making this dream a reality. The house they bought, Drayton Wood, had 35 acres of land, a swimming pool, a tennis court, stables and two paddocks. They purchased a Range Rover, of course. Kitted themselves out in new wellies and Barbours, and filled their property with two dogs (a Great Dane called Moose and a sheepdog named Benjie), two cats (Marmalade and Turbo), three horses (Nobby, Dancer and Lightning), two cows (Bluebell and Thistle) and six geese (I don't remember their names), no partridges and several pear trees.

It was a wonderful place for Lucy and me to visit, and they seemed to adjust well, apart from the occasional mishap. The geese, for example, weren't quite as successful as my father had hoped. 'Geese are great watchdogs, the best,' said my dad.

'What about dogs? Aren't they the best watchdogs?' I challenged.

'No,' my dad insisted, refusing to follow my logic. 'Geese are much better watchdogs than dogs.' So rather than rely on the dogs or indeed install an alarm, he got six geese. On their first night at Drayton Wood, we went to sleep safe in the knowledge the geese would alert us to any unwanted guests by honking. In the morning, we awoke to find six dead geese. My father had forgotten about the food chain. A fox had eaten his new alarm system. It turned out our watchdogs needed watchdogs.

Visiting my dad in the countryside was a real adventure. I had horse-riding lessons, rode my BMX, went swimming, played fetch with the dogs and tennis with my dad. It was the perfect weekend getaway. Holly created her dream country kitchen with copper pots hanging from the ceiling and more herbs and spices than I knew existed. She would prepare a variety of dishes with varying success for our juvenile palates. Regardless of how much we enjoyed it, Lucy and I always reported back to our mum that it was 'disgusting'. Complimenting our new mum's cooking to our real mum would not have been a wise move.

At one lunch, my dad and Holly had several people over. I don't recall the occasion. There must have been about ten of us sitting at the large dining room table. My father at the head, telling stories accompanied by his own booming laugh. I was a child surrounded by adults, so the only time I was involved in conversation I was asked typical questions like, 'What school do you go to?', 'Do you enjoy it there?' and 'What's your favourite subject?'

'Hey, Michael,' asked my dad, 'how are your guitar lessons coming along?'

'You must be a real Jimi Hendrix by now,' Holly added.

I had been bunking off my guitar lessons for a year at this point. It had actually been so long that I had forgotten I was supposed to be going.

My heartbeat quickened, my voice trembled slightly as I mumbled, 'Fffine.'

My dad addressed the whole table: 'Michael begged me to get him a guitar. I wanted him to learn the piano, but he was so adamant.'

'Adam Ant doesn't play the guitar,' interrupted Holly. Everybody laughed at the 'adamant' and 'Adam Ant' mix-up. I thought maybe I was saved and the conversation would turn to New Romantic pop. I was wrong.

'What songs can you play?' asked my dad with a mouthful of Holly's finest 'Sloppy Joe'. I was terrified and tried to change the subject.

'Have you told everybody about the geese? And how you murdered them,' I suggested.

'Oh yes, I will. But first I want to know what songs you can play on that guitar I bought you.'

How was I going to get out of this? I had to remain calm, but my heart was nearly beating out of my chest. I flicked my eyes to Lucy, who knew I hadn't even taken the guitar out of its case. She looked almost as terrified as me.

'Er-er-eeerm,' I stuttered.

'Come on,' reiterated my dad. 'You've been learning the guitar for a year, what's your favourite tune?' All eyes were fixed on me; I felt like throwing up. I couldn't think of a single piece of music ever written.

'The . . .' I began.

'The what?' pushed my dad.

'The National Anthem,' I said finally.

The whole table looked confused. A bit of 'Sloppy Joe' dribbled out of the side of Lucy's mouth. 'The National Anthem?' said my dad, surprised.

'That's very patriotic,' somebody else interjected.

'Yes,' I said, realizing I had some work to do to be convincing, 'I love it, I just love playing it, I love our country, I love the Queen, I'm really good at it. Aren't I, Lucy?'

'Yes,' Lucy assured everyone. 'He's brilliant at it, he plays it all day.'

'OH MY GAD!' interrupted Holly in her thick US

accent. 'Cameron, I can't believe I forgot. I've got an old guitar upstairs in one of the boxes, I'm going to go and get it.'

'What a great idea,' agreed my father. 'After lunch Michael can play the National Anthem.'

The blood drained from my body. I was in hell. I wanted the ground (all 35 acres of it) to open up and swallow me. Holly disappeared to look for the guitar. My mind was racing. What was I going to do? Should I feign illness or injury? I was in the midst of a nightmare. My dad began telling his geese manslaughter story. It seemed like only seconds before Holly returned, tuning her old guitar as she walked towards me. My father cut short his anecdote. 'You found it, great!' Holly placed the guitar in my trembling hands. The whole table turned to me.

'Stand up, Michael,' my father directed.

I stood up, awkwardly holding the alien instrument. This was the moment, the moment I had to admit my lie. The moment to reveal the shameful truth, that I was not so much Jimi Hendrix as the Milli Vanilli of school guitar lessons. I decided to go for it. I don't even know if I decided. I found myself strumming the guitar and singing, 'God save our gracious Queen, long live our noble Queen . . .' I sang it as loud as I could, to mask the fact that I was just randomly strumming. It sounded horrific; my audience looked puzzled.

'EVERYBODY!' I encouraged. 'God save the Queen, de, de, de, de, Send her victorious . . .' Everybody sang along, just about managing to hide my out-of-tune, random guitar-playing. I belted out the last line with lung-bursting pride, like Stuart Pearce at a World Cup: 'LONG TO REIGN OVER US, GOD SAVE THE . . . QUEEEEEN . . . YEAH!' The most embarrassing moment of my life was over. I took a bow and received uncomfortable applause. It turned out I had fooled nobody, and later that night when the guests had departed, my father took me aside. 'Michael, I think we need to talk.'

I wasn't punished for skipping my guitar lessons. My humiliation at lunch was considered punishment enough. Also, my excellent exam results weighed in my favour. I claimed I had been too bogged down with work to learn an instrument.

My dad was pleased with my now glowing school reports. I don't know why but I was particularly good at Latin. I was a 'Latin lover', but not in the sense that pleases women. I was also quite sporty. This might be difficult for you to believe. I opened the batting for the cricket team and was top scorer for the hockey team.

If you think hockey is a bit of a girlie sport, wait until you hear this: my posh private school taught boxing. An ex-boxer, I forget his name, whose face featured the obligatory flat nose, taught us the Queensberry Rules once a week. Fine, you might think. Boxing is good for exercise and co-ordination. Well, at the end of the year a boxing ring was set up in the gym, and there was a tournament when all the parents came to cheer their posh offspring beating the shit out of each other. Come to think of it, with me speaking Latin and boxing in front of a passionate mob, I was like a young Maximus Decimus Meridius in *Gladiator*.

A champion was crowned for every school year. I actually won in the first year, defeating Sam Geddes by a technical knock-out. Sam and I are friends to this day, and I haven't stopped reminding him of my victory for the past twenty-five years. I'm sure he'll be thrilled to learn it's mentioned in my book. I'm sorry, Sam, but the fact is my speed, silky skills and breathtaking power were too much for you. I gave you a boxing lesson. I destroyed you.

In the second year, I wasn't so successful. Maybe after a year as the champ I wasn't as focused. I'd put on a few pounds. I got complacent. 'I could have been a contender.' But I think the real reason I lost was that I fought Ralph Perry in the final. Let me explain what Ralph Perry looked like. Imagine Mike Tyson as a white ten-year-old. I was no match for him. Perry, who later served time for GBH and assaulting a beauty queen, gave me a beating and I lost my crown. I burst into tears when the result was announced and refused to shake Ralph Perry's hand and told him to 'fuck off' in Latin. My dad gave me a long lecture about sportsmanship and told me to use my jab more. But there was to be no rematch. The school woke up to the fact that making kids fight each other was perhaps a bit barbaric and boxing was stopped altogether.

So that just left sports day as the only occasion for my parents to witness my physical prowess. My two sets of parents decided to try to get along 'for the sake of the children'. So my mum, Steve, my dad and Holly chose my sports day as the starting point for their new positive relationship. The venue was Cannons Park, a large sports field set up for athletics. It started well; my four parents were smartly dressed, the sun was shining and the rumour that Patrick Swayze was my dad was going some way to make up for the Kenny Everett debacle of two years earlier. The problem was that this wasn't a dynamic which was going to work. There was far too much resentment, pain and anger between my mum and dad and their new sidekicks. It was excruciating to witness them pretending to get on and fake laughing at each other's jokes.

My event was the long jump and I won. I jumped 3.03 metres, but due to a mix-up the distance was recorded as 3.30 metres. I still would have won, but those extra 27 centimetres meant that I smashed the school record. In fact, I still hold the Arnold House School record for the Under-9 long jump due to this error. Twenty-five years that record has stood. The teachers and headmaster fully expected me to become a professional long jumper. But the time has come to reveal the truth. While I'm in such a confessional mood, I would like to add that I was also on anabolic steroids.

I was so pleased with my record-breaking jump that I rushed into the arms of my dad and then I rushed into the arms of my mum and then I rushed into the arms of my other dad and then I rushed into the arms of my other mum. Then came the surreal fathers' race. It was agreed that both my dads would compete. This was fine by the school, who had encountered this situation before. In fact there were so many additional parents due to broken marriages, they had to run heats.

My dad took his place on the starting line alongside Steve and the other fathers. There was no starting gun, which was a relief because I'm sure at some stage one of my parents would have snatched it and opened fire on the other. Instead Mrs Orton was responsible for starting the race, 'On your marks, get set, shoot!' My dad got off to a bad start, an even worse middle and painfully slow end and finished in last place. Steve won the whole race. My dads had finished in first and last place.

As I celebrated Steve's win, I didn't think about my real dad's feelings. I was too young. Maybe he saw the funny side. It can't have been easy.

But little did I know that in just two more school sports days' time, I would have FOUR dads in the fathers' race (this isn't true).

9

Girls make up half of the population. Girls are what most boys want. There comes a time when a boy's entire life revolves around the pursuit of girls. There are girls reading this book: 'Hi.' I went to an all-boys school. This was a terrible idea. I learned nothing about girls; they were like alien creatures to me. I had such a late start getting to know the fairer sex that it definitely put me at a disadvantage.

I'm not just saying all schools should be mixed; I'd like to go beyond that. I think as soon as you're born you should be shown a girl to begin your education. Then at school you should have to study each other's gender as a subject. 'What's your timetable today, McIntyre?'

'Maths, Geography and then double Girls.'

Also, in addition to French and English, you should be taught 'French Girls' and 'English Girls'. In fact you may as well include 'Latin Girls'; any information about any girl from history can be beneficial in unravelling the extraordinary complexities of females.

Girls, however, probably wouldn't even need one entire lesson in 'Boys', the teacher rounding the lesson off with '... so if they're grumpy, they're probably hungry. OK, girls, we seem to have finished twenty minutes early. So you're free to fiddle with your split ends until break-time.'

I began my phenomenally unsuccessful pursuit of the opposite sex when I was about twelve years old. Sitting outside the school gates on a wall, in her crimson uniform, clutching her violin, was twelve-year-old Lucy Protheroe. She was Christie Brinkley, Princess Leia, Wonderwoman and Princess Aura rolled into one. Lucy's younger brother was at my school and every few days she would collect him and walk to their home just around the corner. From the moment I saw her, it was like a thunderbolt had hit me. The problem was that for her (to continue the analogy), there was no change in the weather conditions; maybe a slight breeze, but nothing more.

I was becoming more independent and had started to take the number 13 or 82 bus from Golders Green to school. These were the old-style London buses, the ones with a conductor and that you just jumped on and off. Nowadays if you miss the bus, the doors close, you curse and you wait for the next one. In those days, you never felt like you'd missed the bus as you could hop on at any time when it stopped in traffic. I would see a bus in the distance in traffic and go tearing after it. It would tease me by always being close enough for me to think I could catch up. I once chased a bus for my entire journey to school.

School finished at 4.30 p.m. and from 3.30 onwards my heart was aflutter at the prospect of Lucy perched on the wall outside. Every day I walked through the school gates and looked to my right to see if she was there. If she wasn't, I would be deflated for a few moments but soon be day-dreaming again about seeing her the following day while sitting on the bus home (or running behind it). If she was there, I would try, and fail, to be cool.

The first problem was the fifty-yard distance between us. I would see her and smile and she would see me and smile. So far, so good. Then I had to walk to her with her staring at me. I knew how to walk, I had been walking for about ten years at that point and had been practising walking throughout my day at school. But I felt so self-conscious under her gaze that my walking skills abandoned me. My normal straightforward walking style was temporarily replaced by a swagger that even Liam Gallagher would have laughed at. I also struggled with direction, often colliding with other people, painfully smacking my hand against a lamp post or brushing along the hedge that ran from the school gate to the wall she was perched upon.

By the time I reached her (covered in leaves and with a sore hand), my mouth would be so dry from nerves that occasionally no words came out at all, just a sound similar to the one a dog makes when you accidentally step on its foot.

We would have an awkward conversation while she would flick her hair from one side to the other. This hair flicking was really quite something. She had fair hair in a bob and would move all of it to one side of her face and then a few moments later flick it back to the other side. I don't know if this was a habit or if she couldn't decide which side looked better; all I know is that it made me look like a tennis spectator, regularly shifting my head to the left and right to follow it. It only added to the hypnotic effect she was having on me.

Between her bobbing hair, she was beautiful. I was fresh-faced, narrow-eyed and chubby. I may not have looked like Matt Goss from Bros but I was determined to maximize whatever attributes I did have. My best feature was, and is, my perfect teeth. The problem is that I don't know if teeth are that high up the list of what girls find attractive. But it's all I had, so I felt I needed to show them off. I would thrust them out of my mouth, like a Bee Gee at the dentist. So I basically looked like a Chinese Bee Gee watching the tennis dressed as a ladybird wearing Kylie Minogue's hot pants. I hoped she fancied me.

She didn't.

We had one 'date'. I flew her to Paris on a private jet and we watched the show at the Moulin Rouge and spent the night at the Ritz. Not quite. We went to the Odeon cinema in Swiss Cottage. Our romance was as successful as the film we saw, *Slipstream* starring Mark Hamill. Exactly. She said there wasn't the right chemistry between us. I was devastated, heartbroken, and blamed my chemistry teacher.

Lucy was just the first in a long list of infatuations with girls that never came to fruition. In fact until I met my wife, Kitty, when I was twenty-two years old, my love life may have been the least successful in history. Teenage girls simply weren't interested in me. Nowadays, I have plenty of teenage girls screaming my name at my gigs, waiting outside and trembling when they meet me. Where were they when I needed them? If only I had released my first DVD when I was thirteen.

When Lucy rejected me, I was heartbroken. 'There're plenty more fish in the sea' tends to be the consoling wisdom of your friends. But it was useless.

'I don't want a fish,' I would squeal with my head in my hands.

'It's just an analogy,' my friends would explain.

'Well, it's a shit analogy, fish stocks in Britain have reduced by 10 per cent due to overfishing, the EU have tried to step in and introduce quotas, but it's no use, I'll never meet another girl.'

That summer I went to Corfu with my best friend Sam, who had forgiven me for beating him in the boxing (it wasn't just a beating, it was a devastating display of my superiority). Sam is properly posh, he's the real deal. He has lords and ladies on one side of the family and royalty on the other. He's in line to the throne, although it would have to involve a lot of unforeseen deaths or a bomb at a Royal wedding he was running late for. I spoke just as 'proper' as him. As you know, my dad was Canadian and my mum from Hungarian stock. I don't have Sam's pedigree, but in his presence I too sounded like an aristocrat.

I've always picked up other people's accents very easily. The problem is that rather than use them as an impression I tended to keep them. Without a doubt I get this from my mum, who embarrassingly takes the accent of whoever she is talking to and starts speaking like that herself. This led to countless cringeworthy scenarios during my youth. If she was in an Italian restaurant and the waiter said, 'Whatta can I getta you?' she would reply, 'I woulda like a Spaghetty Bolognesey anda Garlico Breado, thank you, yes, please.' What made it worse was that she wasn't that good at accents and would sound more like Manuel from *Fawlty Towers*. (I'd like to add that Andrew Sachs, who played Manuel, is a very fine actor, and I'd like to wish him and his family well.)

The worst was when she addressed Pila. Pila was a very sweet little Filipina lady who cleaned our big Hampstead house during the few months we were rich. Pila could barely speak English, so in return, my mum would barely speak English back to her. 'Mis . . . Kati . . . would . . . like . . . me . . . do . . . now?' Pila would hesitantly enquire.

'Pi . . . la,' my mum would respond equally slowly, 'must . . . you . . . now . . . very please . . . do . . . How do you say? . . . Ironing?'

The habit nearly became dangerous in a newsagent's

when my mum was buying some magazines from a six-foot dreadlocked West Indian man. 'Whatsup, Blood,' rapped my mother, 'I is lookin' to buy dis here readin' material, Jah Rastafari.' Luckily Steve and the newsagent were old friends from Brixton, and he managed to diffuse the situation.

So Sam and I went to Corfu sounding like Princes William and Harry. We went with his parents, Hugh and Harriet, his brother Luke and his friend from Eton (wait for it . . .) Quentin Farquar. Hugh always wore corduroy trousers that were one size too small for him, even on the beach. Harriet was lovely jubbly, Luke was like Sam, but older, and Quentin was a perfectly named posh wanker.

I'll never forget Quentin turning to me on the flight and embarrassing me. 'You're quite plebby, aren't you?' he mocked. 'I bet you say things like settee rather than sofa, and serviette rather than napkin, and toilet rather than loo.'

I didn't really know what he was on about. His class teasing made me afraid to speak for the remainder of the flight for fear of saying the wrong thing. In hindsight what I should have said was 'Hey, stupid name snob, what does that say?' and pointed at the 'Toilets' sign on the plane. 'It doesn't say "Loos", does it? Have you got on the wrong flight? This is Pleb Airways, mate. You're fucking with the wrong fake posh boy. Why don't you ask Sam what happened in the boxing tournament?'

When in Corfu, Sam and I were on the hunt for girls or, as Quentin called them, 'top totty' (I think Quentin is probably still a virgin). We both had suntans and Ray-Bans and were feeling confident. Sam's dad rented us a couple of Vespas, and we hit the local town. It was actually more of a historic village. But we weren't perturbed. We had until nine o'clock, our Corfu curfew, and were determined to make the most of it. We scoured the streets. If we had been 'on the pull' for elderly Greek men playing cards, we would have been in luck, but other than them the streets were deserted.

Finally we spotted two similarly aged young girls and devised a carefully thought-out plan of seduction. 'Let's follow them,' Sam suggested. And follow them we did, for about twenty minutes, round and round the village. When they stopped, we stopped. When they continued to walk, so did we. We wanted to be cads but were acting more like private investigators. The problem was that we didn't really have a plan beyond 'Let's follow them.' The two girls then turned and started walking towards us. It seemed like the 'Let's follow them' strategy had worked after all. Sam and I frantically styled our hair as the girls approached. They were surprisingly attractive.

'Bingo,' I whispered to Sam.

The girls halted in front of us and with thick Liverpudlian accents screeched the unforgettable, 'Why the fuck do you think you're following us, you little turds?'

Sam and I had no answer and apologized. 'We're awfully sorry,' we muttered and went home. That was as close as we came to pulling.

Within months, however, I was to experience my first kiss. Doesn't that sound romantic? 'My first kiss.' Well, it wasn't. Sam invited me to a Summer Ball frequented by upper-class-toff teens. It was held at the Hammersmith Palais in London. If you've ever flicked through the pages of *Tatler* magazine and seen the party photos towards the back, you'll know the sort of people who were there. 'Horsey' doesn't come close to describing them. Something happens to your mouth when you speak too posh; it becomes slightly misshapen as if in a constant state of preparation to say something along the lines of, 'Er hillar, jolly good.'

All the Hooray-Henry boys were dressed in black tie, probably in suits passed down through generations of gentry. All the girls were in figure-hugging little black dresses and had names like Arabella shortened to 'Bells' or Pippa shortened to 'Pips'. The object of the ball was to use your odd-shaped posh mouth to 'snog' as many other odd-shaped posh mouths as you could. My mum hired me a suit from Moss Bros and a clip-on bow tie, and I went with Sam and four other cologned young men.

We were dropped off by our parents. 'Have a good time. Don't do anything I wouldn't do,' they hollered, as we disappeared inside clutching our phenomenally expensive tickets. I was nervous and self-conscious. Was tonight the night I would meet the girl of my dreams?

I will never forget the sight that met me when I adjusted my eyes to the Hammersmith Palais lighting. Literally hundreds of under-age upper-class kids with their faces stuck together, 'getting off' with each other. Wow. Maybe it had something to do with them rebelling against their suppressed stiff-upper-lipped lifestyle. Maybe they were just making the most of it until they were carted back to their single-sexed boarding schools. Whatever the explanation my immediate thought was, 'Surely I'm going to pull tonight.'

I turned to express my optimism to Sam only to find him with his tongue already down someone's throat. My other friends also ploughed straight in, mouths open and latching on to whoever was nearest. There are very few things in life as embarrassing as standing next to a kissing couple, so I wandered on to the dance floor and danced, for some time, on my own. Just as I was mid-twist to Chubby Checker's 'The Twist', I saw Sam and another friend, Alex. 'Hey,' I shouted over the music, 'how's it going?'

'Forty-six,' said Alex.

'Fifty-two,' said Sam.

'What? What are you talking about? Fifty-two what?' I genuinely enquired.

'Girls!' they said in unison, now both twisting too.

'You've snogged forty-six and fifty-two girls tonight?'
I asked, amazed.

'Yeah,' said Sam.

'Forty-seven!' said Alex coming up for air from his
latest conquest on the dance floor.

'How many have you snogged, Michael?' asked Sam.

'None,' I admitted. 'How do you do it? What do you
say? Do you say anything? Shall I just start licking someone's face? Help me.'

Sam explained that all he was doing was approaching
girls and asking whether they wanted to go and sit
down. This was code for 'snog'. They would then take
a seat together and he would rack up another digit on
his tally.

'Go for it, Michael. Find a pretty girl and ask her if
she wants to sit down with you on one of the sofas,'
Sam encouraged.

'Really?' I said. 'That's all, just ask if she wants to sit
with me on one of the settees?'

'Sofas!' Sam corrected. 'You're such a pleb.' And with
that, he disappeared.

I now felt I had more purpose. I saw a space open up
on one of the sofas and scanned the dance floor. And
there she was, without a doubt the best-looking girl at
the ball. 'That's her,' I thought. 'I'd rather kiss her than
a hundred of the others.' I twisted over to where she
was dancing as Chubby Checker continued to sing.
'How long is this song?' I thought. 'It must be the long

version.' She had dark hair and beautiful green eyes and fitted perfectly into her obligatory little black dress. It was as if she was the only girl on the dance floor, the only girl in the world. My heart was pounding. I moved in closer, a bit too close. I moved back a bit. I caught her eye.

'I would like to go and sit down.' I fluffed my line. Rather than ask her to sit down, I had simply informed her of my own movements. She looked at me, puzzled. I quickly tried again: 'Would you like to come and sit down on the sof-tee with me?'

This was better. At least it was a proposition of some kind. However, I had forgotten whether sofa or settee was the correct thing to say and ended up creating my own chair, the sof-tee. I corrected myself again: 'The sofa. Would you like to sit down with me on the sofa?'

There it was, the big question. It was out there. I'm not exaggerating when I say it took her some time to come up with an answer. She literally mulled it over, looking me up and down as I continued twisting to a record I was now convinced was stuck.

'All right, then,' she finally said.

I'd pulled!

Just.

Together we found a vacant slot between two other sets of snoggers. She was gorgeous, smelled wonderful and her perfect lips were attached to a perfect mouth, not like the back pages of *Tatler* at all. We sat down, she took out her chewing gum and within moments we were kissing. In the middle of the Hammersmith Palais surrounded by girls of loose morals, I had finally found one loose enough to kiss me. The sensation of kissing for the first time was extraordinary. Our tongues met with all the passion of a Magimix. Hers was swirling round and round, so mine did the same, chasing it. There was so much swirling that we started to froth a bit and my saliva was in danger of becoming stiff peaks. Then it was over. I thanked her, way too much; she returned the chewing gum to her mouth and stood up to leave.

'What's your name?' I asked, worried I would lose her for ever.

'Izzy,' she said.

'Easy?' I questioned. Just my luck, the only girl I can pull is actually called 'Easy'.

'No,' she said, 'Izzy, short for Elizabeth.'

And then she was gone.

Sam's final total was ninety-one and Alex's eighty-seven. Mine was one. But I didn't care, because I was convinced she was 'the one'. I was in love with her. I told my four friends that I had kissed the most beautiful girl at the ball. They seemed happy for me. 'Her name was Izzy,' I told them through my perma-grin.

It transpired that they all knew Izzy. They'd all snogged her that night. I was just a number on her tally. It was also the common consensus that she wasn't a very good kisser. 'Kissed like a blender,' somebody said.

I had to agree. I was deflated, but not for long. I was off the mark. Surely things could only get better now. I had a newfound confidence. I had blender-kissed some chick called Izzy, and now I was a player. I had experience.

The next time I saw Lucy Protheroe sitting on the wall outside my school, I played it super-cool. No problems walking the fifty yards now.

'Hi, Michael, how have you been?' she asked, between hair flicks.

'Good,' I said. As if I couldn't care less.

'Are you going to the disco?' she asked.

The major event on the school calendar was the Arnold House Disco. All the local girls' schools were invited, and the gymnasium was transformed into a discothèque. I'd been dreaming about this night for ages. But I played it cool.

'Maybe,' I said with more nonchalance than I knew I was capable of.

She seemed intrigued by my cocky persona.

'What have you been up to?' she asked.

'Snogging,' I coolly announced.

'What? In school?' she probed.

'No, me and my friends went to a ball the other night, and let's just say . . . I got a little bit of action,' I said, trying to make her jealous.

'Oh, the one at the Hammersmith Palais. I can't believe you went to that. That's for, like, the poshest people on earth. Apparently everyone snogs everyone, it's gross. I know a girl called Izzy went and snogged, like, every boy there. But I'm glad you met someone, what's her name? Where does she go to school?'

My face went bright red as I looked for an excuse to leave. A National Express coach drove past us.

'I'd better go, that's my bus,' and I ran after the coach.

'Where are you going, Michael? . . . That's a coach . . . to Birmingham . . .' she cried as I sprinted after it.

All week the school was buzzing at the prospect of this year's school disco. I was thirteen years old and in my last year at Arnold House. I went shopping with my mum for my outfit and ended up opting for a fluorescent red shirt. I can't remember where we bought it; all I remember is that it glowed in the dark, and I truly believed that my increased visibility would give me the edge over my male rivals. One of my mother's friends' daughters, Jessica Taylor, was also going, so my mother organized her to be my 'date'. Before you get excited and think I may have 'pulled' before I even got to the disco, let me just explain that Jessica was 6 foot 3 inches and had a thick moustache.

Steve had a new 'company car' that David Rosenberg had given him to replace the written-off BMW 6-Series. It was a black Ford Orion 1.6i with 'new car' smell. It was a balmy summer's night, a perfect opportunity to use the sunroof which came as standard. Steve and I picked up my 'date', Jessica, and he chauffeured us to the disco. I sat in the back with my red shirt glowing, and Jessica sat in the front with her head sticking out of the sunroof, her moustache blowing in the warm wind.

It was so weird arriving at school at night. I looked at Lucy's empty wall in the crepuscular (surely the most impressive word I've used so far. It basically means dim) light. I was so over her. As soon as I shake off Jessica, I'll have the pick of all the girls in the Borough of Camden. Jessica and I put our coats away and nervously walked into my school gymnasium, the sound of Wham!'s 'Wake Me Up Before You Go-Go' getting louder with every step. The gym was unrecognizable; there was a glitter ball, flashing coloured lights, and smoke pumped out of a smoke machine. Nobody was dancing. All the boys were camped out in one corner and all the girls in the opposite corner. I looked up to Jessica's face; the lights were reflecting off my fluorescent shirt making her moustache look like it was on fire. Almost in unison we said we wanted to find our friends. So we each took our places on our respective sides of the gym.

There must have been about fifty boys and fifty girls. I hooked up with Sam and my friends. 'What the fuck are you wearing, McIntyre?' Sam said (in fact, everyone said that). 'Who do you fancy?' asked Sam gesturing towards the girls camped in their corner. There they all were. Fifty thirteen-year-old girls of all different colours and creeds and shapes and sizes; it was like an advert for Benetton.

I saw Lucy Protheroe. I could cross her off the list, so there were forty-nine potentials. They all looked pretty in their own way, all dressed up in their new dresses. Even Jessica looked quite attractive until she got her hair tangled up in the basketball net. I had my eye on one girl who was wearing a Madonna-inspired ensemble complete with white lace gloves. When the DJ put on 'Ghostbusters' accompanied by some strobe lighting, she had a mild epileptic fit and had to be picked up by her parents. Down to forty-eight; they're dropping like flies. Someone's got to make a move and ask one of them to dance.

Apparently Rick Astley's 'Never Gonna Give You Up' was what many of the boys were waiting for. By the second verse, the middle of the gym was filled with boys and girls awkwardly dancing with each other. Jessica was dancing with Watson (the smallest kid in the class, who hid behind the blackboard) – that was quite a sight.

But, as usual, I was on my own. My confidence from the Izzy kiss was over, and here I was again, a bundle of nerves. Asking a girl to dance requires a tremendous amount of courage. The fear of rejection is too much to bear. I didn't know if I could take it. There are two different forms of school disco dance. There's the straightforward dancing opposite each other for the length of one eighties upbeat song, or there's a slow dance. A slow dance is, of course, dictated by the tempo of the track playing. A normal dance is relatively trivial, but a slow dance involves bodily contact. Which at that age is quite intense. A slow dance is the Holy Grail of the Arnold House school disco. A girl may accept an invitation to dance to, say, Billy Ocean's 'Caribbean Queen' but refuse a slow dance to Terence Trent D'Arby's 'Sign Your Name'.

Soon the boys' side of the gym and the girls' side were no longer distinguishable. Everyone was dancing with each other and enjoying themselves. I could barely dance. Because we were in the gym, I got confused and started squat-thrusting and doing star jumps, I think at one point I said the Lord's Prayer. There was one girl I liked, but thought she was out of my league – and anyway my old electric-guitar-playing friend Gary Johnson was dancing with her. He was the coolest boy in school – what chance did I have?

Before you give up hope in me, I can tell you that I did pluck up the courage to ask a girl to dance. As the DJ played the Bangles, I walked like an Egyptian until I was standing directly in front of Alison with her dark frizzy hair and welcoming smile. 'Do you want to dance?' I asked confidently.

Just as she opened her mouth to agree, the lights darkened and the music changed to Gloria Estefan's 'Can't Stay Away from You'. It was too late, she'd agreed. My timing was spot on. The dance floor cleared of girls who weren't willing to take their 'dancing' relationships to the 'slow dance' level, leaving just a handful of us.

I'd like to just clarify what a slow dance actually entails. Alison and I were holding each other's hips and stepping from side to side. The song finished, and Gloria Estefan was aptly replaced by 'Don't Stop Believin'' by Journey. Alison wasn't all that keen on me and quickly disappeared, but it didn't matter. I was a hero. Everyone had witnessed our dance. My friends, and boys I barely knew, patted me on the back: 'Nice one, McIntyre.' I was proud that I had found the courage and succeeded, even though Alison may only have been a victim of excellent timing on my part.

There was one person that night who sent every girl in the gym into a flutter. Pulses racing, blushed faces, what a hunk. With timing even better than mine, Steve walked in to collect me as 'The Time of My Life' from the *Dirty Dancing* soundtrack played. There wasn't a single girl at the disco (or mother collecting their child) who didn't want to run into his arms and attempt 'the lift'.

My Alison dance was as good as it got for me that night. It could have been worse. I just wasn't one of those boys whom girls had crushes on. I knew I was different. I was a funny kid, in more ways than one. But even from such an early age, I was obsessed with finding my girl. I wasn't interested in all girls. I wanted my one. I always felt incomplete, like I was missing someone, someone to love and to bring out the best in me. I knew she was out there somewhere, just not in the Arnold House School gym.

But she was.

Dancing with Gary Johnson was Kitty Ward. The love of my life, my wife and the mother of my children.

It would be nearly ten years until we met.

IO

My teens had begun. I had two dads, two mums, one Date, one Slow Dance, one Snog. My boxing record was one Win and one Loss. I held the Under-9 long jump record, was an experienced voice-over artist and a keen 'fake' guitar-player. Oh, and I was destined for fame and fortune according to a Tarot card reader in a now closed down spiritualist bookshop in Kensington.

I left Arnold House and headed to a public school called Merchant Taylors' in a place named Northwood, outside London in Middlesex. My parents thought it would be good for me to go to a school in the sticks, lots of beautiful grounds, sports and fresh air. It took me ages to get there, and when I got there, I hated it all day, then it would take me ages to get back. Everyone else at the school lived locally in suburbia. There were 150 boys in my year and I couldn't stand any of them. They were all the same to me. Boring. There's a Billy Connolly routine when he mentions how the real characters in life are the very rich and the very poor, but everyone in the middle is dull. That's what the boys at Merchant Taylors' were. Middle. They were middle class and lived in Middlesex and destined to be working in middle management with a middle parting, driving a middle of the range Audi in the middle lane.

I had no real friends. Not a happy time for me, made worse as I was beginning the long and painful transition from boy to man, commonly known as puberty. Why it has to take so many years, I have no idea. There's a classic scene in the film *An American Werewolf in London* when he first changes into a were-wolf. He collapses on the living room floor and, while screaming in agony, his body changes shape with hair sprouting out of it. The whole scene lasts about forty seconds. As painful as it looks, I wish puberty hap-pened like that. Exactly like that. Even with the soundtrack. The song 'Bad Moon Rising' by Creed-ence Clearwater Revival should be cued up on the family stereo of every teenager in the world. As soon as they feel shooting pains in their body, they must rush to the hi-fi and press 'play', then drop to their knees and transform into an adult. That's where the analogy must end; they shouldn't then go on a killing spree and wake up naked in London Zoo.

As it is, this excruciating maturing of your body is spread over several years. I wasn't even aware of puberty. It never crossed my mind that my body had a lot of growing up to do and nobody mentioned it. My mother and father failed to tell me anything at all during this time. I think they left it to each other, but because they weren't on speaking terms, they didn't realize I was still in the wilderness. I never had the chat about 'the birds and the bees'; in fact, for many years, I thought that birds and bees had sex with each other.

So it was a bit of a shock when my body experienced its first changes. Hair appeared under my arm. Not both arms, one arm. I had hair under one arm for almost a year. My left arm. I appeared to be going through puberty from left to right. I was half man, half child. I was all set to become a Greek mythological figure.

Once a week we had swimming. Changing for swimming was a chance for all the boys in my class to catch up with each other's various rates of development. Some kids had experienced no changes whatsoever. I had my hair under my left arm, other kids had hair under both arms, or pubic hair or both, or a little wispy moustache or a small gathering of hairs on their chest. Everybody was at different stages. Everybody except for Panos Triandafilidis, the Greek kid, who was so hairy, it was difficult to see where his foot hair, leg hair, pubic hair, chest hair, facial hair and nose hair began and ended. He had hair in his ears and on his back; I think I saw a couple of strands on his eyeballs. When he walked near soap, it would automatically lather. He looked like early man. Early man, that is, with a girl's voice as his voice hadn't yet broken.

My voice took years to break. For years I sounded exactly like my mother. Every time we picked up the phone at home, callers would get us mixed up. A classmate of mine once called, my mum picked up and they had a five-minute chat about Latin homework. Steve once phoned from work, I picked up and he told me he couldn't wait to come home and have sex with me.

The worst part of all these hormones running around my body was my spots. I would go so far as to say acne. I would get horrendous clusters of spots appearing anywhere on my face. Just when one would leave, another would show up. My face looked like a pepperoni pizza with extra pepperoni. What really wound me up were the products like Clearasil that were supposed to help. The advert would say, 'It gets rid of your spots in just four days.' Just four days? Four days is the amount of time it takes for a spot to heal on its own. Spots last four days if they are untreated. So all Clearasil does is make you stink of Clearasil.

I, of course, made things even worse than that for myself. I chose 'skin-tinted' Clearasil. What you may have noticed from looking at the faces of your fellow human beings is that they all have different-tinted faces. There isn't one skin shade for all. I'm sure there's some-one in the world with the exact skin tint as the skin-tinted Clearasil. This product is like a miracle for them; they put it on their face and the spots literally disappear behind this medicinal product that's working hard to rid their face of the hidden blemishes in just four days. Unfortunately for everyone else, and me, the skin-tinted Clearasil makes you look worse than before. I would wipe this beige goo all over my spots, leaving me with what looked like bits of somebody else's face on my face; and it stank.

There was also a dandruff situation. Mine was by no means the worst in the school. There were so many white speckles on school blazer shoulders that when my grandmother came once to watch me play cricket she thought it was part of the design. All this came at a time when I first started to have sexual desires. Before adolescence, girls were soft and made me feel funny inside; now, I wanted to ravage them, a lot.

Unfortunately, these new feelings coincided with me looking horrendous. I would see girls from local schools on the overground Metropolitan Line Tube I took to and from school. I had hair under one armpit, spots covered in skin-tinted Clearasil occasionally with dandruff stuck to it and the voice of a posh girl. I was so embarrassed by my appearance that I would dread any schoolgirls getting on the same carriage as me. I would seriously panic that the species I was so desperate to attract would literally laugh at my appearance.

Every day I took the fast train to school. The fast train missed out certain stations. It was fun to see the other teenage school kids waiting on the platform thinking the train was going to stop and then jumping out of their skin-tinted skin as we whooshed past. The trains were pretty old and rattly. When the train reached its top speed, the sound of the rails screeching was deafening and the passengers would be bouncing up and down in their bench-like seats. I preferred the fast train, not because it was quicker, but because it didn't stop to let in teenage schoolgirls. The only stop between Finchley Road, where I got on, and the school, Northwood, was Harrow-on-the-Hill.

Sorry, I'm going to interrupt myself because I've just remembered a little story about Harrow-on-the-Hill. I was once trying to get there on a bus and I asked the West Indian bus conductor where the bus was going. 'Herne Hill,' he said. Herne Hill is nowhere near Harrow-on-the-Hill. But if you say Herne Hill with a West Indian accent (try it) it sounds exactly like Harrow-on-the-Hill. So I ended up in Herne Hill.

Anyway, as I was writing. My biggest fear when stopping at Harrow-on-the-Hill was realized one morning when, as I was sitting alone, about fifteen loud, gum-chewing, hair-twiddling, hoop-earring-wearing girls got on and sat all around me in their green uniforms with shortened skirts and green tights. I was so embarrassed I went bright red, which only served to highlight my skin-tinted Clearasil even more. The loudest of the girls had cheap make-up and her hair was pulled back so tight in her shocking pink scrunchy, it looked like she'd given herself a facelift. She stared directly at me, I immediately turned to look out of the window. 'You're well ugly, intya,' she said while her friends all cracked up laughing at me bouncing around as the train picked up speed. I would have felt more comfortable playing the National Anthem on my guitar on top of Buckingham Palace at the Queen's Jubilee.

My confidence was at an all-time low. Even in sexual matters concerning only myself I managed to fail (brace yourself for this). At some time during puberty, boys start to masturbate. Deal with it. If you're a young boy reading this, thank you for taking the time out of your hectic masturbation schedule to read my book. If you're an even younger boy, this is all still to come (so to speak), and if you're a parent, please knock before entering your son's bedroom. Now, as I have previously mentioned, my parents never discussed any sexual developmental matters with me. I have also mentioned that at Merchant Taylors' I didn't really have any close friends. The net result was that I didn't know what 'wanking' was.

I started, due to nature, to get erections. My fellow students would talk endlessly about 'wanking'. I came to the conclusion that wanking meant to have an erection.

So I was constantly getting erections and doing nothing with them. I thought that I was wanking. My vulgar classmates were often chatting about their own masturbation and borrowing each other's pornography. 'I wanked three times last night', 'Can I borrow your wank mag?', that kind of thing. A classmate once pointedly asked me, 'Do you wank, McIntyre?'

To which I responded, 'Yeah, all the time,' thinking he

was referring to getting erections, 'I wake up wanking.'

'You wake up wanking?' he said incredulously.

'Yeah, always. I wanked this morning on the train. I wanked for most of Geography. My mum had people round for dinner last night, and I couldn't stop myself from wanking the whole way through it,' came my shocking response.

Of course, the more I didn't attend to these erections, the more frequent they became, until soon they became permanent. I was walking around with a permanent erection. I telephoned my friend Sam, who now went to Westminster School in central London. Although I was embarrassed, I knew Sam would have some answers.

This was obviously before the days when all teenagers had a mobile phone, but I was lucky enough to have a phone in my bedroom. Although you wouldn't know it was a phone because it looked like a Ferrari. There was a shop on Golders Green Road that sold gimmicky phones, and as a family we embraced them. The phone in the hall was a frog, and the phone in my mum's room was a piano. I should probably update you on the décor in our home and how my mother's taste was developing in the nineties. The house was very colourful. Pastel colours. Every pastel colour there is, clashing with each other. All the rooms had different-coloured carpets from each other and from the hallways and from the walls that had different colours from each other. It was as if she'd

looked at the Dulux colour chart and said, 'I can't decide,
let's have all of them.' So I called Sam on my Ferrari
phone.

'Hello?'

'Hi, Sam,' I said.

'No, darling, it's Sam's mum. Do you want to speak
to Sam?'

'Yes, please,' I said.

'Sam! Telephone!' I heard her call.

'Hello?' said Sam, collecting the phone.

'Hi, Sam,' I said.

'Oh, hi, is that Michael's mum?' Sam replied.

'No, it's me, Michael.'

'Hi, Michael, how are you?'

'I've got a bit of an embarrassing problem, and I don't
know who to talk to. Can you talk privately?' I asked.

'Yeah, what is it?' Sam said.

'I can't stop wanking,' I confessed.

'Me neither. So what?' said Sam, as if it was no big
deal.

'I don't think you quite understand, Sam, I literally
cannot stop wanking. I wank all day long,' I continued.

'Michael, it's normal. Don't worry. It's natural.
Everyone's doing it, whether they admit it or not,'
Sam reassured.

'OK,' I said, starting to feel a bit better. 'But I think
I'm doing it more than anyone else. Like when we have

swimming at school, I'm the only one wanking in the changing rooms.'

'You wank in the changing room! When you're changing for swimming!' Sam exclaimed. 'What? Like in the loo, while everyone else is changing?'

'Yeah,' I admitted. 'And also when I'm walking around,' I continued, 'and in the pool.'

'You wank while you're walking around! You wank in the pool!' Sam said, revolted.

'That's what I'm trying to tell you, Sam. I can't stop. I'm wanking right now.'

Sam hung up.

My problem only lasted a couple more days before (I'll be delicate) there was an eruption. All on its own, untouched by me. It's how the story of Adam and Eve would have been if there was no Eve. Suddenly it all made sense. My embarrassing mistake was realized, and I am proud to say I haven't masturbated since (this may not be true).

As you can imagine, home life was turning into a disaster. I was hormonal, snappy and ugly. For some reason, rebelling against your parents is part of growing up. Your parents give you life, feed you and clothe you, and then you turn on them in your teens. I would come home from school with my tie half undone, my shirt hanging out of my trousers and my skin-tinted Clearasil smudged on my face.

'Hello, darling, how was school today?' Mum would ask.

'Fuck off, I hate you, I hate you!' I would scream before running upstairs to my bedroom and slamming the door behind me.

I was a nightmare to live with. I committed all the domestic teenage crimes. My mother constantly accused me of 'treating the place like it was a hotel' because I would never tidy my room, I'd leave my clothes on the bathroom floor and steal her towels when I went out.

I was a repeat offender at eating without getting a plate. I would stand at the fridge, grazing on whatever took my fancy, grabbing clumps of ham and dipping them in the mayonnaise jar.

'Michael! What are you doing? Get a plate if you want to eat something,' my mum would demand as she walked into the kitchen.

'Fuck off, I hate you, I hate you!' I would scream as little bits of mayonnaisey ham spluttered on her face, before I ran upstairs to my bedroom and slammed the door behind me.

I feel I need to update you on the relationship between my mother and Steve. While I was skipping my guitar lessons at Arnold House, bouncing around on the Metropolitan Line and walking around with an erection, they were married, and my mum had been pushing out baby boys at an alarming rate. I have three brothers, Nicholas, Thomas and Andre. Technically they are half brothers, so officially I have one and a half brothers. They were like Russian dolls. Not because they were smaller than each other and looked alike, but because they all look like fat Russian girls. That's a joke. They were probably the best part of my teenage life, just like my kids are the best part of my life now. It's wonderful to have innocent new people crawling and toddling around.

I apologize particularly to Steve for my behaviour during these years. If a teenager rebels against their parents, I can tell you, rebellion goes up a notch with a step-parent. Steve made an enormous effort with me, but it was no use, I could barely look at him. Before puberty Steve was a cool bonus dad, resisting my stomach punches and winning at my sports day. Now he was just this bloke living with us, in my face. Get out of my face. Who are you? You're not my dad.

He never reacted to me and I must have pushed him right to the edge. Many lesser men would have reacted. There was one moment when, looking back, he says he was close to breaking point. After months of behaving appallingly, I went down to the kitchen for a drink. This normally involved standing at the fridge and drinking out of a bottle or carton. I was wearing a dirty old T-shirt and my boxer shorts the wrong way round. I opened the fridge and scanned the contents. I couldn't see anything I wanted, so I had a good rummage around. Steve then entered the kitchen to be met with the sight of me bending down. Now, you know that little opening on the front of boxer shorts? Well, that was now at the back and wide open due to my bending.

'Oh, for fuck's sake!' Steve exclaimed.

'There's nothing to drink,' I moaned with my head in the back of the fridge.

'Do you know that your arsehole is on display?' Steve asked in disgust.

'What!' I quickly stood up, knocking my head on the shelf, spilling yoghurt on my hair and covering the back of my boxer shorts with my hands. After countless teenage strops and tantrums, this could have been the final straw. Steve walked out muttering to himself about how he couldn't take much more. But he didn't (for want of a better word) crack, and he never did. Not with me anyway.

As I've previously mentioned, Steve is a remarkably good-natured man. My teenage shenanigans weren't enough to derail his passive personality. He never even raised his voice. But it soon transpired Steve did indeed have a breaking point. One average summer's day he was driving my mum in the BMW 3-Series with their two toddlers Nicholas and Thomas (Andre wasn't born yet) in baby seats in the back. I should mention the car is the same 3-Series as before and was now so old that actual grass was growing on the floor. Grass. Growing in the car. I don't know if this has ever happened to another car. I remember the day when my mother announced the phenomenon and the subsequent debate over whether to cut it or add an herbaceous border.

Anyway, so Steve was driving to or from a spot of shopping in Temple Fortune when a car full of yobs pulled up alongside our moving garden. They started hooting to get attention, and making lewd gestures and suggestive remarks to my mum. Make no mistake, these thugs were wild-eyed and dangerous. My mother told them to fuck off, but Steve calmed her down, not wanting to encourage them. He tried to manoeuvre the car away from the ruffians but ended up directly behind them in traffic. My mum was rattled, but luckily the kids in the back were pretty much oblivious to the unsavoury incident.

The traffic started to move, and Steve began to pick up speed when the hoodlums in front braked suddenly, deliberately forcing him to do the same. He screeched to a halt. My mother reached in front of Steve to hoot them, but Steve again felt it would only encourage them to respond. The traffic moved once more, and again the villains in front braked hard, forcing Steve to do the same. This time the whiplash hurt one of the kids, who started crying. The yobs in front were swearing and laughing. The situation was getting tense. They had to get out of there.

My mum was hysterical and scribbled down the licence plate of the ASBO wannabes and told Steve to drive immediately to the police station, for their own safety as much as to report the incident. Steve remained ice-cool. He managed to drop back in traffic and reach the police station without further trouble. They got out of the BMW. My mum, still shaken, lifted the kids out of the car. Steve then spotted the culprits sitting in traffic a little further down the road.

'There they are,' said Steve methodically.

'Quick, Steve, get in the police station!' my mum implored.

'Wait here,' Steve said in an unfamiliar voice and with a look in his eyes she'd never seen before. Only one person had seen this look before, the bully who locked him in the cupboard on his first day at school. My mother screamed for him to come back, but it was no use. Steve sprinted down the road at fathers' race-winning pace.

There were four of these youths in the car. Late teens/early twenties. They were hoodies in the days before hooded tops. Their eyes lit up at the prospect of a fight as Steve knocked on the driver's window. The driver rolled down the window: 'Yeah! What the fuck do you want, mate? Do you want me to get out of this car and beat the shit out of you?' threatened the driver, with the rest of the car chipping in with similarly articulate intimidation. But Steve wasn't there to engage in macho posturing. Steve had reached breaking point and, although they didn't know it yet, that was bad news for them.

Steve grabbed the driver by the throat and ripped him out of the car window. He then lifted him up off the ground and issued a few basic suggestions about how he might wish to behave in future. The three other thugs got out of the car but, rather than confront a man who pulls other men out of car windows with one hand, made a run for it. Steve dropped the driver on to the road and received deserved applause from fellow drivers and elderly Jewish ladies who had abandoned their Danish pastries to come outside and witness the kerfuffle.

From then on, I was a little bit more respectful around the house and always made sure my boxer shorts were the right way around when bending.

My real father and Holly also married, a lovely summer wedding with the reception at Drayton Wood. And they too produced children of their own, Billy and Georgina, another half-brother and half-sister for me. Bringing my total to one sister, one half-sister and four half-brothers (the equivalent of one and a half sisters and two brothers).

But their love affair with the English countryside soon ended and they moved to Los Angeles. They sold Drayton Wood with its 35 acres of land, swimming pool, tennis court, stables and two paddocks. They sold the Range Rover, their wellies, their Barbours, their two dogs (a Great Dane called Moose and a sheepdog named Benjie), two cats (Marmalade and

Turbo), three horses (Nobby, Dancer and Lightning), two cows (Bluebell and Thistle), no partridges and several pear trees. And my dad sold his BMW 635 CSI.

I can understand the lure of LA. Holly had been living there, the sun shines every day, and it's the home of showbusiness. England, however, was the home of his children and leaving us was heartbreaking for Dad. I tried to convince him not to leave England's green and pleasant land and sang the National Anthem (unaccompanied this time) as he packed his suitcase. I remember him telling me over and over again how he loved me and how leaving Lucy and me was the most difficult decision of his life. In truth, I didn't feel abandoned. You can't miss something you never really had in the first place. We led separate lives. We only saw each other every other weekend – that was simply not enough time for us to have a proper relationship.

The plan was for Lucy and me to spend our school holidays Stateside with our dad. The first time I went to California, I had to agree it had the edge over Hertfordshire. My dad and Holly bought a beautiful Spanish house in the Hollywood Hills. It had an enormous swimming pool, a guesthouse, a trampoline, a grand piano and celebrity neighbours. Holly drove a Chrysler Station Wagon, and my dad bought a new Jaguar. My father started a video production company making music videos, and Holly opened a children's clothes shop called Lemonade Lake. Lucy and I loved it. We went to Universal Studios, Disneyland and Sea World, rode the biggest rollercoaster in the world at Magic Mountain, but best of all spent quality time with our dad. For the first time since Hampstead, it felt like we lived with him.

I want to get across to you how special a time we had together on these trips to America, so I'm going to write it as a cinematic comedy montage. Cat Stevens's 'Father and Son' plays as we see:

Scene 1: We're bouncing on the trampoline together, giggling. Dad bounces into the sitting position, which leads to me being bounced high into the sky and landing in a tree. We both laugh hysterically and I cling to the branches.

Scene 2: We're cruising down Rodeo Drive in my dad's Jaguar. He opens the sunroof. I squirt the windscreen fluid which projects through the roof and into his face. We both laugh hysterically.

Scene 3: We sit next to each other on Colossus, the highest rollercoaster in the world. The car slowly ascends to its full height and then tears downwards, twisting and turning at high speeds. It comes to a halt. We both vomit and then laugh hysterically.

Scene 4: We're playing ball in the garden. He's wearing an American football helmet and throws an American football, cut to me dressed as a cricketer. I hit the ball into next door's garden. It hits a sunbathing John Travolta in the head. We laugh hysterically.

Scene 5: We're sipping hot chocolate with marshmallows and watching a movie before bed. I'm in my pyjamas and he's in a dressing gown with the word 'Dad' written on the back.

Cat Stevens fades out.

During my trips across the pond, I really embraced the American way of life. I became an all-American kid overnight. I loved baseball, I told everybody to have a nice day and I put massive amounts of weight on my arse. I actually became obsessed with baseball. I passionately supported the LA Dodgers. I watched all the games on TV and can still name all the players, who invariably had names tailor-made for the over-the-top American commentators, my favourites being Darryl Strawberry, Pedro Guerrero and Orel Hershiser.

The highlight of my first trip was when my dad and I went to Dodger Stadium to watch a game. The Dodgers were clinging on to a 1-0 lead when it was the turn of Danny Heep to hit. Danny Heep wasn't a regular in the team. I had never seen him hit the ball once. In my three weeks of following baseball, I had concluded that Danny Heep was useless. I turned to my dad and said, 'Danny Heep is shit.'

To which my dad said, 'Heep of shit.' He then proceeded to chant, 'HEEP OF SHIT, HEEP OF SHIT, HEEP OF SHIT.' Before long the crowd surrounding us started to join in, 'HEEP OF SHIT, HEEP OF

SHIT.' My father's unsupportive jibe was spreading around the stadium. Soon the entire Dodger Stadium was chanting, 'HEEP OF SHIT', including the other players, children and even Danny Heep himself (I may be exaggerating). Heep naturally struck out and returned to the dug-out. My dad and I laughed hysterically.

My father continued to smoke constantly. As any wife would be, Holly was worried about his health. Her idea to stop him smoking was to start smoking herself. Her theory was that he would be so worried about her health that they would both quit. This, of course, backfired, and she too became a heavy smoker. But when they weren't coughing, they seemed deliriously happy, and so were Lucy and I on our visits.

One of the most powerful memories of my early teenage years was how I felt when I returned to England knowing it would be six or nine months until I saw him again. This was the first proper pain I had experienced in my life. I didn't feel heartache when my parents got divorced. I didn't miss my dad when I only saw him at weekends. I didn't even feel particularly upset when we said our goodbyes in Los Angeles. I was excited to get home to see my mum and little brothers. But when I got back to Golders Green and I was wide awake in the middle of the night with jet lag, I yearned for him. I missed him so much.

My bedroom was in the converted loft, and I would creep downstairs to find Lucy in exactly the same state as myself. Crying and longing for our dad. There was a lot of talk by both our parents through the years about how decisions were made for the best – logical, reasonable arguments about how life would be better this way – and most of the time I agreed. You just get on with life, that's how you survive. But in the small hours of the morning, after every visit to America, the true raw reality of my parents' separation broke my heart.

Wow. That was a little heavy. Let's lighten the mood and turn our attentions to the loss of my virginity. Strap yourselves in. So as I've already told you, I wasn't the most attractive teenager. Girls didn't fancy me, they laughed at me on trains. By the time I was sixteen I still hadn't added to my one blender-kiss at the Hammersmith Palais. I didn't know how to pull girls; for a while I didn't know how to pull myself. Opportunities were limited. I had no real friends at Merchant Taylors' but had remained close to my Arnold House friends.

Like everyone else at that age, Sam was totally obsessed with sex. He was, however, more overt about his obsession than most. He had a library of pornography. His bedroom walls were covered in pictures of tits. I, on the other hand, had no pornography. I was too embarrassed to borrow any or, God forbid, buy any. The most titillation I got was watching Felicity Kendall bend down to do some weeding on *The Good Life*.

That was until we became one of the first households in the country to get Sky TV. When we had Sky TV, they only had one advert on it, for Eagle Star Insurance, which they played over and over again. (It worked, incidentally, as I now have my home insured with them.) The satellite receiver was in my mum and Steve's room, and they ran a cable to my room so that I could watch the cricket from the West Indies through the night. This set-up meant that the channel could only be changed from the receiver that was in a cupboard next to Steve's side of the bed. The thrill of early satellite television for me was not the Test Match, but the German gameshow *Tutti Frutti*, which featured girls stripping between standard fingers-on-the-buzzers Q and A. It was in a language I didn't speak and the picture quality was poor, but *Tutti Frutti* was the best show I had ever seen.

Getting to watch *Tutti Frutti* was not easy. I had to sneak into my mum and Steve's bedroom while they were asleep, open the cupboard that was less than a foot from the sleeping Steve. The channel would invariably be on number 11 as they tended to fall asleep watching Sky News. I had to change it to 47, RTL. I couldn't just press 4 and 7; that sophisticated channel-changing technology was still at the prototype phase. I had to flick individually through all the channels, 12, 13, 14, 15, 16 . . . until 47. The tension was unbearable, but the thought of German tits kept me focused.

Occasionally Steve or my mother would stir or there would be a noise from the street outside. I would be startled and rush back to my bedroom, only to find I had not yet reached the magic number 47. I may only have reached number 22, the History Channel, or even 46, the National Geographic Channel; interesting, informative and educational they may be, but not the visual stimulus for what I had in mind. So I would return later to complete my mission. I did this every night. I think I watched every episode of *Tutti Frutti* ever made. I even started to enjoy the game play element, and when Hans Schneider was crowned champion, I was genuinely chuffed for him. Hilariously, after a few weeks an engineer came round to look at our Sky Box because Steve had complained to customer services that there was a fault. 'It keeps changing itself to some weird German channel during the night.'

'I'm sorry, sir, it's a mystery,' said the engineer. Well, the mystery ends here.

Sam and I had tried following girls in Corfu without success, but now we had a new plan. We would go to a nightclub. We scanned the clubbing section of *Time Out* magazine and selected a trendy hotspot just off the King's Road. The major stumbling block was that we were two years underage. I was sixteen and looked younger. My most adult feature was the hair under one armpit. I thought of trying to comb it across to the other side or cutting one sleeve off a shirt to reveal my manliness, but it would be no use. There was just no way we could pass for eighteen. Sam looked even younger than me.

'Sam, there's just no way we'll get in. You've got to be eighteen,' I said, deflated.

'That's not a problem. I know somewhere we can get fake ID,' Sam replied confidently.

This was a tremendously thrilling and illegal prospect. Fake ID could open up the entire adult world to me. A world I was desperate to gain entry to. Thank God for Sam, he's so cool, so well connected. We'll hook up with his contacts at MI5 who will furnish us with new passports, new names, new identities. Identities of eighteen-year-olds, eighteen-year-olds who have sex. I'm going to have sex as a fake eighteen-year-old with a new name.

Maybe I could select a name that might help me seduce women, like Don Juan or even David Juan, Don's older brother who taught him everything he knew. I could choose the name of a dynasty synonymous with wealth, like Kennedy or Getty or Rothschild. I could choose a family name that has become a successful brand, like Cadbury, Ford or Guinness. I could be a Freud or a Von Trapp. The possibilities were endless and exciting. After much deliberation, I decided to keep my first name. Michael was a name I was used to. I liked it and I was worried that if I changed my name to, say, Jake, I might confuse myself unnecessarily. I imagined myself dancing in a nightclub just off the King's Road when a gorgeous eighteen-year-old girl approaches: 'Hi, it's Jake, isn't it? I want to have sex with you.'

'No, I'm Michael, I think you've got the wrong guy,'

I reply. 'No, wait, I actually am Jake, look, look at my fake ID, I mean ID.' I couldn't risk it.

So it was decided my new name would be Michael Casio-Sony. I decided to take advantage of my oriental looks and pretend to be heir to both the Casio and Sony empires after my mother, Kati Casio, married my father, Ray Cameron Sony, in a ceremony that started precisely on time and where the music for the first dance was listened to on Walkmans.

'Where are we going to get the fake ID from?' I asked Sam.

'The YHA,' Sam said.

'The what?' I questioned.

'The YHA, the Youth Hostel Association,' Sam explained.

'What is that?' I asked.

'It's the association of youth hostels, what do you think it is? You just join up and fill in your details and apparently they then give you a card with your details on,' Sam explained.

'How does that help us?' I was genuinely confused.

'You don't give them your real details, you give them a fake name and date of birth, and then they give you a card with whatever you told them written on it. Bingo, fake ID.'

It might not have been the passport issued by Q from James Bond that I was hoping for, but it seemed worth a shot. Although I was worried that even if the nightclub bouncer believed we were eighteen, did he really want to let in people who were members of the Youth Hostel Association, was that really the kind of clientele this trendy hotspot was looking for? I wanted to look like someone who was going to be drinking cocktails and chatting up girls, not someone seeking shelter.

Sam and I headed down to YHA headquarters in central London and joined the massive queue of foreigners lugging enormous backpacks. I bought my passport-size photo and filled out my form with the key lies. Name: Michael Casio-Sony, D.O.B: 21/2/1974. When I finally reached the front of the queue, I handed over my false information and, just as Sam had said, it was instantly processed with no questions asked. Within minutes, we were both fully fledged YHA members. With a bit of luck, we would be handed cards to use as fake ID to get into nightclubs, and as an added bonus, if we pulled, we could take the lucky ladies to over 20,000 youth hostels worldwide.

We were indeed handed official-looking YHA memberships that displayed our photos, our new names and ages. So far, so good. Unfortunately, the membership card was an enormous piece of paper, about A4 size. It was basically a certificate. But we had queued for most of the day, we'd come this far, it was too late to back out. We went home to freshen up and negotiate our curfew with my mum. We checked *Time Out* magazine; the club opened at 9 p.m. and closed at 3 a.m.

'Mum?' I asked within moments of arriving back. 'Can Sam and I go to the cinema tonight?'

'Sure. What's on? Do you want me to drive you?' helpfully asked my mum, forever trying to be nice to her bolshie, hormonal sixteen-year-old.

'No, thanks, we'll take the Tube,' I said.

The word 'thanks' was a mistake. I don't think I'd used it since the first hair appeared under my left arm-pit. She knew something was up.

'It's quite a long film, so we might be home quite late, please.'

Please? What was wrong with me? I was completely malfunctioning. That 'please' didn't even really fit into the sentence.

'What time?' my mum asked sceptically.

'I don't know, midnight, maybe later,' I said, pushing my luck.

'Michael, you have to be home by eleven. That's the rule. That's more than enough time to see a film, and if it isn't, see another one. I know you're up to something, so whatever it is, be back here by eleven o'clock.'

'Fuck off, I hate you, I hate you!' I screamed before running upstairs to my bedroom and slamming the door behind me.

Sam and I plotted our evening. It takes forty-five minutes to get back home from the King's Road, so we would have to leave the club at 10.15 p.m., which leaves us with one hour and fifteen minutes of clubbing time.

We'll have to make them count. I perused my wardrobe. What to wear? What will make beautiful King's Road chicks fall at my feet?

I knew nothing about fashion. I still don't. If I had done, I would have known that my outfit selection was putting me at a severe disadvantage in the pulling arena. My grandma had bought me a beige T-shirt covered in prints of African elephants. I knew it was expensive, so I thought it must be cool. Just the kind of thing the heir to two electronics empires would wear. Jeans have never suited me; in case you're wondering why – then imagine me in jeans. Go on, do it now . . . See what I mean? So I opted for cords. Brown ones. Little did I know then, but it has since been scientifically proven that it is impossible for a woman to be attracted to a man wearing brown corduroy. So with my brown cords and African elephant T-shirt, what better way to complete the ensemble than with a pair of black loafers? Believe it or not, I did look in the mirror before I went out and thought I looked good.

We were concerned about the club being very busy, so we arrived half an hour early so that we might be first in the queue. We needn't have worried. Nobody, literally nobody, apart from Sam and me in 1992, has gone to a nightclub at the opening time. Most clubbers show up at midnight or later, but there we were loitering on our own at the entrance at 8.30 p.m. It was still light. At 9 p.m. our big moment came. Two burly bouncers (is there any other kind?) were standing outside as Sam and I confidently strode up to the entrance.

'Are you open?' Sam said, his voice breaking on the words 'are' and 'open'.

The bouncer couldn't help himself from chuckling as he saw the pair of us.

'Do you want to come?' he asked.

Nerves overcame me, which, as you know, results in me becoming extremely posh.

'Yes, please, we want to come into this night establishment,' I said.

'Night establishment?' the bouncer asked. 'How old are you two?'

'Eighteen,' we both said in unison, practically before he'd finished asking the question.

'Have you got any ID?' the bouncer pressed.

This was the moment we had been preparing for all day. We instantly whipped out our A4 YHA certificates. The bouncer scrutinized them. He didn't seem to be perturbed by the size or nature of them, he just checked the information. Sam's name and birth date on his fake ID were both strokes of genius.

'That's today's date. It is your birthday today, David?' the bouncer asked Sam.

'Yeah, it is, mate,' Sam replied in an odd cockney accent.

'Happy birthday,' the bouncer said, seemingly genuinely. 'David Kray, any relation?'

'Yeah, leave it, will ya?' Sam confidently revealed.

Now, in my opinion, there's no way on earth that the bouncer believed him. I think he just admired his audacity – so much so that he let us both in. Sam and I got into the hottest club in London with our fake IDs, at 9 p.m. We paid the exorbitant entrance charge and took a look around. What we found was an empty nightclub. The music hadn't even started yet. There was a barman cleaning glasses and another man mopping the floors. We took further advantage of our fake IDs and drank a Malibu and lemonade each, but the scene in the club hadn't changed by the time we had to go. We were the first to arrive and the first to leave.

Our clubbing adventure did not produce the results I was hoping for. Although I think even if we had stayed until three in the morning, Michael Casio-Sony wouldn't have had much luck with the ladies. The problem was the clothes on my body and the spots on my face. But, as if by magic, these problems would disappear. On holiday. On holiday you don't really wear clothes. As long as you don't wear Speedos, and I didn't, it's difficult to go too far wrong. Also the sun had a miraculous effect on my skin. It cleared my spots up almost entirely and made me much better-looking. In fact I tanned quite well, which would bring out my blue eyes. I had been doing endless sit-ups in my bedroom, a bit like Robert De Niro when he was incarcerated in *Cape Fear*. So I was in good shape, the best shape of my life, it would turn out. Put simply, after three or four days on holiday, I was gorgeous.

That summer Lucy and I were not visiting our dad, as we would be spending Christmas with him instead. So I organized some serious summer vacationing. It kicked off with a two-week family holiday in Malta with Lucy, my mum, Steve, Nicholas and Thomas (Andre still not born). Then Sam and I were Interrailing around Europe. Our itinerary was as follows: London to Paris, Paris to the South of France, where Sam had relatives and we had friends, South of France to Monte Carlo to meet up with my grandma (Helllo, daaarling) and Jim for a few days, South of France to Switzerland, where Sam had a royal relative living in a castle, Switzerland to Italy, where we also had a friend to stay with, and then Italy to home. I set off with my rucksack, my passport, my Interrail ticket, some travellers' cheques and my virginity. During that summer I lost my rucksack, my passport, my Interrail ticket, some travellers' cheques and on the very last day I lost my watch. I'm kidding. I lost my virginity. Unfortunately, losing my passport was about as pleasurable.

It came to the last day of my summer. I had visited four countries and one principality without closing the deal. But now on the final night of our adventure, I was odds-on for some nookie. I had met a French girl in Malta; her name was Sandrine and she was reasonably attractive in the right light, more attractive still in no light. We shared some passionate moments at night on the beach in Malta. We'd reached second, maybe third base, using the popular baseball analogy. Continuing the baseball analogy, I would say that both of our techniques were as accomplished as the hitting skills of Danny Heep. She was also a virgin. Not ideal. I've always felt that life would be so much easier if boys were shown the ropes by an older, more experienced woman. I would actually make it compulsory, like jury duty. Single women in their late thirties should be assigned a teenage boy each. They would be sent a name and address in the post and they have six months to have sex with him or face jail time. This is probably a bit extreme (although I bet there are some single women in their late thirties totally up for the idea).

Anyway, after a lot of nocturnal fumbling in Malta, we said an emotional goodbye and exchanged details. It turned out she lived in Calais. Who lives in Calais? Does she live in the port? Is she a ferry driver? Regardless, this was good news for me, as I would be passing this port, with my passport, twice over the coming weeks. So when it came to the last day of my trip and my virginity was intact, Sam and I decided to stop off at her Calais residence. Sam provided me with sexual tips. Embarrassing as it may be to admit, he even drew me a diagram on a napkin of areas to aim for on the female form. 'Make sure you talk to her, girls love it. Tell her how beautiful she is, compliment her,' Sam advised.

'But she isn't really,' I admitted.

'That's not the point, this is your first time. You have to start somewhere, and girls need to be coaxed, they need to be turned on. Listen to me, or it will be a disaster,' Sam continued.

When we arrived at Calais train station to be picked up, the scene was tremendously awkward. Sam and I spoke GCSE French, and Sandrine and her parents spoke Baccalauréat English. This worked quite well at the beginning, but we soon used up all our phrases in the car journey.

'Hello, how are you?', 'What is your name?', 'My name is Michael', 'How old are you?', 'Can you tell me the way to the train station?', 'Why? We've just come from the station', 'What time is it?', 'I would like some bread.'

The last ten minutes of the journey passed in silence until her father said, 'This is our home.'

To which I said in French, 'Where do you live?'

Waiting for us was Sandrine. She was hairier than I remembered. I wondered if she might be related to Panos Triandafilidis from Merchant Taylors'. She was pleased to see me, she liked me; I just wished she liked deodorant as much. She had a friend with her who was much better-looking. Sam swooped instantly. Sandrine showed me around her sweet home. Strangely, her parents went out, encouraging me to take their daughter's virginity. Sam also disappeared, with the hottest girl in

Calais. 'I told you I had a girl in every port,' he said as they left. 'Remember,' he whispered, 'compliment her.'

She showed me to her bedroom. It was neat and tidy and had views of the Channel. We sat on her bed, with my diagram in my pocket, and shared a bottle of duty-free wine and giant Toblerone from the local booze-cruise supermarket. I was a little freaked out by a shrine she had constructed in her room. It was a shrine to the few days we spent together in Malta. It was a bulletin board that had the note with my address on it as well as the tickets from a disco we went to and photos of us together. This was obviously the moment. I couldn't not close this deal. She had a shrine. To me. In her bedroom.

I don't want to go into too much detail, but by the third mountain of giant Toblerone I made my move. We started kissing and undressing. Sam had briefed me on the potential stumbling block of the bra strap. Rather than risk an awkward hiccup, he had equipped me with nail scissors which I subtly removed from my back pocket and cut clean through the strap behind her. Bravo. It worked a treat. I went swiftly though first, second and third bases, but I was nervous, so I then went back to second base, then back to first base, then to third. What kind of a baseball game was this?

This was probably the most nervous I had ever been in my life, which, of course, made me super posh when I followed Sam's advice to compliment her. 'You have quite the most beautiful . . .' I scanned her for her best feature. She had pretty good legs. I was all set to say 'legs' when I noticed this enormous birthmark on one of her thighs. So I decided to say 'leg'. But then I thought, 'I can't, I can't say, "You have the most beautiful leg."' I ended up saying 'room'. 'You have quite the most beautiful room.' She didn't seem to mind that I'd overlooked everything about her and commented on the scenery.

In fact, she loved it. '*Merci, merci, Michel.*' It really got her going.

This encouraged me. 'I'm particularly fond of your lamp; is it antique?' Things moved swiftly from here. Before I could comment on her rug (the one on the floor), I found myself at home base. I'd scored. It lasted no more than about three minutes (still a record for me) and afterwards I felt like a man. At last.

I lit one of her duty-free Gauloises cigarettes and looked out of her bedroom window as the sun set over England.

'I'm coming home. I set sail tomorrow. Lock up your daughters!'

In retrospect, I think saying this out loud was disrespectful.

12

My main priority on my return home was not to lose my tan. I was a tanned, sexually active man, and I wanted it to stay that way. Nature dictated that my tan would gradually fade. Every day I was becoming paler, and my spots were returning. My newfound power to attract girls who make shrines to me in their bedroom was leaving me. However, I was determined to fight nature and purchased some Clarins fake tan. I now had a fake tan and fake ID. I was the real deal. Unfortunately, my application of the Clarins fake tan was far from expert and, in my haste to darken my face, I forgot about my neck. This was OK while I still had the remnants of my real tan, but when that disappeared, I had a face that looked like it had just got back from two weeks in the Caribbean and a neck that looked like it had just got back from two weeks in Glasgow. To say that I was teased about this at Merchant Taylors' would be an understatement. I claimed that I fell asleep sunbathing in a polo neck, but nobody believed me, and I was soon forced to admit that my bronzing was fraudulent. I then seemed to have even fewer friends there than the zero that I had before.

Unbeknownst to me, my days at Merchant Taylors' were numbered. I was in my first year of A-Levels and, despite my failure to connect socially with anybody there, I was settled. I had worked hard and done well in my GCSEs (five As and four Bs) and was studying Biology, Chemistry and Geography for my A-Levels. I didn't particularly enjoy these subjects, but I was pretty good at them. They weren't vocational; I didn't plan on becoming a doctor or a weatherman. I opened the batting for the cricket team and was top scorer in the hockey team. I had less than two years remaining, and then I suppose I planned on going to university like everyone else. But then, totally out of the blue, in the middle of term, in the middle of the week, my father telephoned. We normally spoke on Sundays, so his phoning was irregular.

'Hi, Dad, what's up?'

'Are you sitting down?' my dad said, seriously.

It seemed like such an odd question. Nobody had ever said anything like that to me before. He was going to tell me something that could potentially make me fall over. What could this collapse-worthy news be? Anyway, I wasn't sitting down.

'No, I'm not, I'm not sitting down. Shall I sit down?' I was intrigued by this whole sitting-down thing.

'I think you should,' my dad confirmed, keeping the same serious tone.

I was speaking on the frog phone in the hall. There was nowhere to sit.

'There's no chair here. Shall I sit on the floor?' This conversation was getting weirder and weirder.

'If you want, Michael, sit on the floor,' my dad agreed.

I sat cross-legged on the carpet.

'OK, I'm on the floor now, Dad, I'm sitting on the floor. What is it?'

'Michael, I'm very sorry but you have to leave your school. I'm in serious financial trouble, and I simply can't afford to pay the fees any longer. I'm so very sorry, I know you're happy there. I've tried very hard to find a solution, but I can't.'

When my parents split up my father had agreed to pay school fees for Lucy and me. Lucy went to Henrietta Barnett, one of the best state schools in the country that was conveniently located less than a mile from our home, but my dad still had to fork out a small fortune to send me to a school nowhere near my home so that I could be surrounded by characterless, suburban twats and one suspected paedophile.

At this point my dad had been in America for about five years. His explanation for things not working out was that in England he was a big fish in a small pond but in the States he was a small fish in a big pond. When you also consider he had to cross the pond to get there, you can see the kind of nightmare he was having. He had been ripped off by one of his partners at his video production company in LA and Holly's shop, Lemonade Lake, hadn't been as profitable as hoped. They had

downsized in LA before moving north to the breath-
takingly beautiful state of Vermont. There they had
opened another Lemonade Lake, this time selling toys,
and lived a much simpler life. So there was little income.
The Range Rovers, BMWs, Jaguars, swimming pools,
tennis courts, farm animals and trampolines were over.
Showbusiness is tough and unforgiving and my dad
was now in his early fifties. If only he had stayed in
London and been a comedy exec at the BBC – but he
chased a dream in America and it backfired.

I wasn't devastated at all. I needn't have sat on the
floor. In fact I wished I hadn't, as I got quite bad pins
and needles and when I moved I cried out in pain. My
father misinterpreted this and thought I was taking the
news very badly. The only thing that did upset me was
that his paying my fees was one of the few links I had
to him. I had an argument with him the previous year
when he suggested that I went to a state sixth-form college. 'You'd have to give me the money for the fees,' I
said. He was unbelievably upset by this remark, but it
was not born out of greed. I didn't want his money; I
wanted to feel like he was giving me something.

I hated my school, and the prospect of taking my
brown face and white neck out of there seemed quite
exciting. My mum and dad had apparently been in cahoots
over this for a while. This wasn't a maybe, it was happen-
ing, now. Merchant Taylors' were aware of the situation,
and I had an interview the following day at a local state

sixth-form college in Finchley. I was moving to state school. I wish it had been filmed, as it would have made for a hilarious Channel 4 fly-on-the-wall documentary.

Let me tell you a bit about the school life I was accustomed to. I wore a uniform with a tie representing my 'house' called Hilles. There were school 'houses' who played each other at sport and had meetings and such. When the teacher entered, we had to stand up and say, 'Good morning, sir' or 'Good afternoon, sir.' The teachers wore black cloaks that wafted behind them as they walked. The headmaster wore all the gear. He had several cloaks and a big hat, so his authority was in no doubt.

I had no idea what was appropriate to wear to the interview at Woodhouse College. I suggested to my mum that I wear my Merchant Taylors' uniform without the tie. She told me to look smart, so I donned my elephant T-shirt, cords and loafers. My brother Nicholas was at nursery, but Thomas was still a baby so he had to come with us. Our appointment with the headmaster was at 11 a.m. We arrived in good time with Thomas conveniently sleeping in his pushchair.

The college was a lateral, not unpleasant Georgian building. Inside, it was much like you would expect, modern, sterile, functional, cheap. My mum and I sat on seats not designed for comfort outside the headmaster's office. I was nervous. Waiting outside any headmaster's office is nerve-wracking.

At five minutes to eleven, the headmaster's door

opened. My heart skipped a beat. False alarm, it was a man in a tracksuit top. It must be the gym teacher.

'Hello? Michael, is it? If you're early, then we might as well start,' he said, kindly.

Good Lord, it was the headmaster. In a tracksuit top. What kind of a place was this?

My mother and I stood up to the shared relief of our bottoms. Thomas was still soundly asleep in his push-chair. I decided to break the atmosphere with a joke. 'I hope you don't mind,' I said to the headmaster, 'but I brought my wife and child along.'

This, I repeat, was a joke. I thought that was obvious. Apparently not for the headmaster of a state school that teaches sixteen- to nineteen-year-olds.

'That's absolutely fine, Michael,' said the headmaster, 'many of our students have kids here.'

Unbelievable. Where was I?

The interview went so well that at the end he said he was not just happy to accept me into the college, but also offered me the position of English teacher.

So within days of taking my father's phone call while sitting cross-legged on the carpet, I was starting at a new school. This time nervousness did not make me posh, it made me mute. Everybody else had started at the college about six weeks earlier, they had made friends and formed cliques. I was a late entrant, the new guy. I took the same number bus I used to take, but this time in the opposite direction. When I arrived for my first day, the scene was a far cry from the samey Merchant Taylors' pupils. The major difference was that the lack of school uniform meant the students could express themselves at a time in life when they were extremely keen to express themselves. Every fashion statement ever made was being made by someone, and every race, creed and colour was represented. When I got inside the main building, it resembled the departures lounge of an international airport.

I kept my head down and kept quiet. I was terrified, but already enjoying it more than Merchant Taylors'. The exciting difference from what I was used to was girls. Girls, girls, girls, everywhere. Small ones, big ones, white ones, black ones, brown ones, tall ones, short ones, blonde ones, brunette ones, ginger (strawberry blonde) ones, a bald one (what's going on there?), too-much-make-up-wearing ones, not-enough-make-up-wearing ones, and one with the biggest breasts I had seen in my life. Wow. I was mesmerized by them. These were knock-out knockers. They were attached to a long dark frizzy-haired beauty. I was lost. Asking directions is an ice-breaker. It could lead to something.

I opened my mouth to speak, but as I hadn't spoken for so long my throat was dry and no words came out, just this bizarre croak. She looked at me, bemused. I cleared my throat and tried again.

'Hi, I'm looking for room 42,' I said finally with the clarity I'd initially hoped for.

'Room 42?' she said with a voice that seemed to perfectly match her tits. 'Just down the hall and I think it's the second left.'

Our exchange did lead to something. It led to room 42. I'd hoped for more, but, hey, I had plenty of time. I went to school here, with hundreds of girls. This knowledge suddenly gave me a rush of confidence, and I decided to take our relationship to the next level.

'What's your name?' I asked.

'Tina,' she said.

I stood there for a few moments waiting for her to ask mine. She didn't. I headed to room 42.

I found room 42. My classroom. When I entered, the scene was so rowdy that nobody noticed the new boy. It was a large class of about thirty-odd. People were laughing, play-fighting, chewing gum, throwing bits of paper, smoking, breastfeeding. I took a vacant seat right at the back next to a stocky bloke with two gold earrings in one ear and a shaven head.

'All right, mate?' he said in a voice that seemed to perfectly match his hair and earrings.

'Yes, mate, I'm fine, dandy.' I had never used the word 'dandy' before in my life. What a time for it to make its debut.

'You're posh, innit?' he asked.

There's really no answer to this question. So I decided to ask one of my own.

'What "house" are you in?' I asked, referring to the school 'house' system at public schools.

He just stared at me, trying to make sense of my question before saying, 'Yeah, I like a bit of house, but mainly hip-hop and ragga.'

At that moment, the teacher walked in. I had met him briefly when I came in for my interview. I immediately bolted to my feet and exclaimed at the top of my voice, 'GOOD MORNING, SIR!'

Nobody else in the class reacted when the teacher walked in. But they certainly reacted to me. They all stopped laughing, play-fighting, chewing gum, throwing bits of paper, smoking, breastfeeding and turned to stare at me.

I was baffled why they weren't standing to attention and presumed they hadn't noticed the teacher had entered.

'Sir's here,' I whispered to my new classmates.

'Who?' a few of them mumbled.

'Sir!' I repeated, motioning towards the teacher. At this point, even the teacher looked behind him, wondering who I was referring to.

So this tremendously embarrassing misunderstanding is how I introduced myself to the class. People were confused by me, as if I was an alien from the Planet Posh. That didn't really change much as people got to know me. Woodhouse was all about cliques. The mass of differences I witnessed arriving on my first day soon turned into groups. There were probably more, but the ones I remember are: 'The Goths', 'The Asians', 'The Jews', 'The Rockers', 'The Greeks', 'The Geeks' and me. Initially I joined 'The Asians' (maybe it was my Clarins fake tan).

They auditioned me for their clique by inviting me out to lunch. At lunch, most people went to North Finchley High Road. I suggested PizzaExpress. They laughed. We went to the kebab shop and bonded over doners. A week previously I was at a school like Hogwarts but without the magic, and now here I was eating kebabs with Dilip, Chirag, Ammet and Jeet on North Finchley High Road. I felt out of place in both settings. I always felt out of place, but at least I was in a new place, and the kebabs were amazing.

Not long after I started at Woodhouse, it was Valentine's Day, the day for lovers and for wannabe lovers to make their intentions known. Valentine's cards are traditionally sent anonymously, signed with a question mark. Great lot of use that is – you have no idea who fancies you; for all you know it's the Riddler from *Batman*. My new college was filled with posturing boys and blushing girls waiting to make a move on each other. This was the perfect opportunity.

An internal post bag was set up for students to send each other cards. I wasn't particularly hopeful of receiving any, but when the bag arrived for my class on

Valentine's morning, it was so overflowing I thought I might be in with a shout. As it turned out, every single card, and there must have been close to a hundred, was addressed to the same guy. The school stud, Karim Adel. He accepted his teen heartthrob status with nonchalance and even handed out some of the cards for his fellow classmates to open on his behalf. I opened a few and they didn't just contain question marks, they were shockingly graphic essays of desire.

I didn't understand it. I looked closely at Karim; I needed to be like him. What did he have that I didn't? Well, for a start, he was Iranian. There was nothing I could do about my heritage. We were of similar height, similar build, I definitely had better teeth, but the main difference was his shoulder-length hair. In fact, one of the saucier cards I read made several references to Karim's hair. So I decided to grow my hair and imagined myself one year on when the next Valentine's postbag was delivered. Karim and I would be sitting next to each other with our long hair intertwining and bathing in a sea of Valentine's cards addressed to us.

Growing your hair isn't easy. Because hair grows upwards, you have to wait until it reaches a certain length and weight before gravity kicks in and it falls nicely over your shoulders – 'Because I'm worth it!' Before that, it will look unkempt and unattractive – 'Because I'm not worth it!' During this difficult middle phase, I bought a cap and squashed my overgrown hair inside. Soon the cap couldn't contain the growing locks and they would sprout out of the back and on the sides. When I removed the cap, my hair would shoot up vertically.

While I was waiting for my hair to grow, a new opportunity to attract girls presented itself. I had started driving lessons and on one of her Sunday visits, my grandmother announced she wanted to give me some money to buy my first car. She was like a fruit machine: every once in a while you'd hit the jackpot. She gave me £2,000 to buy whatever car I wanted. I was so excited. My own car. Freedom. Every day I scanned the pages of *Loot*, *Autotrader* and *What Car?* to find my dream set of wheels.

Quite a few of the students had their own cars and drove to college. They would park adjacent to the school in a parade of the worst vehicles on the road, like a queue for the crusher at the car pound. I wanted a car that would stand out and turn heads. In particular the head of Tina, the girl I met on my first day who had her own airbags to compensate for the lack of extras on whatever car I could afford.

What is the coolest car you can buy for £2k? It was like a challenge on *Top Gear*. I stumbled across the 'Classic Cars' section of *Loot*. I hadn't been checking there as I assumed classic cars cost a fortune. But there she was. There was no photo but the particulars sounded amazing: Triumph Spitfire Mark IV, Royal Blue, con-